The Giant Schnauzer Club Handbook 2010 has been produced for all those enthusiastic about this truly magnificent breed. The Club has been running for just over 30 years; officially registered on 1 November 1979, The main objective being to promote and encourage the best interests of the breed. With this book comes an invitation to join us and support the Giant Schnauzer into the future.

By The Giant Schnauzer Club

Published by the Giant Schnauzer Club Oct 2010
Illustrations by Lesley Parker

© Copyright the Giant Schnauzer Club

All rights reserved. No part of this book may be used or reproduced without written permission from the publisher. For permission please contact the Giant Schnauzer Club Secretary.
Email: secretary@giantschnauzerclub.co.uk

ISBN 978-0-9566817-0-6

Printed and bound in the UK by the MPG Books Group, Bodmin and King's Lynn

Officers & Committee
2010

www.giantschnauzerclub.co.uk

President: Mrs Kari Wilberg

∘◆∘◆∘◆∘

Acting Secretary: Mrs Karen Carroll
248 Oxcliffe Road
Morecambe
Lancashire
LA3 3EH
01524 411220
secretary@giantschnauzerclub.co.uk

∘◆∘◆∘◆∘

Treasurer & Membership Secretary: Mr James Parker
treasurer@giantschnauzerclub.co.uk
membership@giantschnauzerclub.co.uk

∘◆∘◆∘◆∘

Committee:
Mr Lloyd Eyre (Committee Chairman)
chairman@giantschnauzerclub.co.uk

Mrs Heather Smith (GSC Welfare)
rescue@giantschnauzerclub.co.uk

Mrs Lesley Parker (Assistant Secretary)
assistantsec@giantschnauzerclub.co.uk

Mr Robert Smith
Mr Kirk Moss (Co-opted)

Contents

The Breed Standard	7
Illustrated Breed Standard	10
History of the Giant Schnauzer	20
The Giant Schnauzer in Britain (1987)	25
The Giant Schnauzer in Britain Update (1998)	30
The Giant Schnauzer in Britain Update (2010)	31
The Pepper and Salt Giant in Britain (1987)	40
The Pepper and Salt Giant in Britain Update (1998)	43
The Pepper and Salt Giant in Britain Update (2010)	44
The Working Giant Schnauzer	48
Giant Schnauzer Registrations 1971-2009	54
UK Giant Schnauzer Champions	55
UK Giant Schnauzer Imports	85
Evolution of the Giant Schnauzer on the European Continent	111
Choosing a Giant Schnauzer	114
Dog Breeding Check List	122
Keeping Our Breed Healthy	123
Showing Your Giant Schnauzer	125
Supreme Champion Philippe Olivier	127
Giant Schnauzer Welfare	130
Grooming, Clipping and Trimming	132
List of Advertisers	138

Giant Schnauzer Breed Standard
Courtesy of the Kennel Club · Last Updated September 2007

A Breed Standard is the guideline which describes the ideal characteristics, temperament and appearance of a breed and ensures that the breed is fit for function. Absolute soundness is essential. Breeders and judges should at all times be careful to avoid obvious conditions or exaggerations which would be detrimental in any way to the health, welfare or soundness of this breed. From time to time certain conditions or exaggerations may be considered to have the potential to affect dogs in some breeds adversely, and judges and breeders are requested to refer to the Kennel Club website for details of any such current issues. If a feature or quality is desirable it should only be present in the right measure.

General Appearance
Powerfully built, robust, sinewy, appearing almost square. Imposing, with keen expression and alert attitude. Correct conformation of the utmost importance.

Characteristics
Versatile, strong, hardy, intelligent and vigorous. Adaptable, capable of great speed and endurance and resistant to weather.

Temperament
Bold, reliable, good-natured and composed.

Head and Skull
Head strong, of good length, narrowing from ears to eyes and then gradually toward end of nose. The overall length (from nose to occiput) is in proportion to the back (from withers to set on of tail) approximately 1:2. Upper part of head (occiput to base of forehead) moderately broad between ears - with flat creaseless forehead. Well muscled but not over-developed cheeks. Medium stop accentuated by bushy eyebrows. Powerful muzzle ending in a moderately blunt wedge, with bristly stubby moustache and chin whiskers. Ridge of nose straight, running parallel to extension of forehead. Nose black with wide nostrils.

Eyes
Medium-sized, dark, oval, set forward, with lower lid fitting closely.

Ears
Neat, V-shaped, set high and dropping forward to temple.

Mouth
Jaws strong with a perfect, regular and complete scissor bite, i.e. upper teeth closely overlapping lower teeth and set square to the jaws. Lips black, closing tightly but not overlapping.

Neck
Moderately long, strong and slightly arched, skin close to throat, neck set cleanly on shoulders.

Forequarters
Shoulders flat, well laid back. Forelegs straight viewed from any angle. Muscles smooth and lithe rather than prominent, bone strong, carried straight to feet. Elbows set close to body and pointing directly backward.

Body
Chest moderately broad and deep, reaching at least to height of elbow rising slightly backward to loins. Breast bone clearly extends to beyond joint of shoulder and upper arm forming the conspicuous forechest. Back strong and straight, slightly higher at shoulder than at hindquarters, with short, well developed loins. Slightly sloping croup. Ribs well sprung. Length of body equal to height at top of withers to ground.

Hindquarters
Strongly muscled. Stifles forming a well defined angle. Upper thighs vertical to stifle, from stifle to hock in line with extension of upper neck line, from hock vertical to ground. When viewed from rear, hindlegs parallel.

Feet
Pointing directly forward, short, round, compact with closely arched toes. Deep, dark and firm pads. Dark nails.

Tail
Previously customarily docked. Docked: Set on high and carried at an angle slightly above topline. Customarily docked to two joints. Undocked: Set on high and carried at an angle slightly above topline. In balance with the rest of the dog.

Gait/Movement
Free, balanced and vigorous, with good reach of forequarters and good driving power from hindquarters. Topline remains level in action.

Coat
Top coat harsh and wiry, just short enough for smartness on body. Slightly shorter on neck and shoulders, but blending smoothly into body coat. Clean on throat, skull, ears and under tail. Good undercoat. Harsh hair on legs.

Colour
(a) Pure black (b) Pepper and salt: Shades range from dark iron grey to light grey; hairs banded black/light/black. Dark facial mask essential, harmonising with corresponding body colour. On both colours white markings on head, chest and legs undesirable. Good pigmentation essential.

Size
Height: dogs: 65-70 cms (25½ -27½ ins); bitches: 60-65 cms (23½ - 25½). Variations outside these limits undesirable.

Faults
Any departure from the foregoing points should be considered a fault and the seriousness with which the fault should be regarded should be in exact proportion to its degree and its effect upon the health and welfare of the dog.

Note
Male animals should have two apparently normal testicles fully descended into the scrotum.

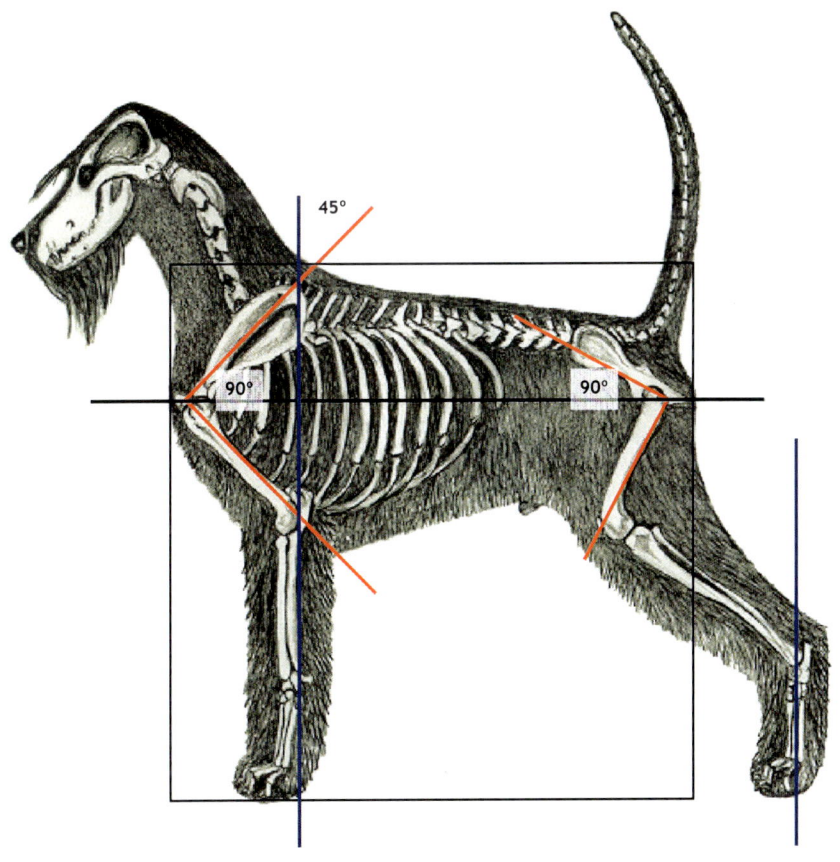

Illustrated Breed Standard

Dentition

There are 20 upper teeth and 22 lower teeth in the adult Giant Schnauzer. Puppies are born with no teeth but deciduous teeth begin to appear at 3 to 4 weeks of age. In total a puppy will cut 28 "milk" teeth. At about 3 months of age, the permanent teeth start to erupt and displace the deciduous teeth. By the time puppies are 7 months old all permanent teeth should be present.

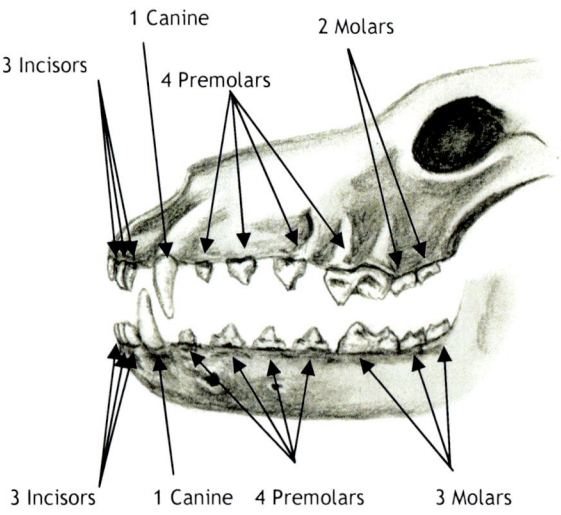

Normal Scissor Bite - the top teeth should closely overlap the bottom

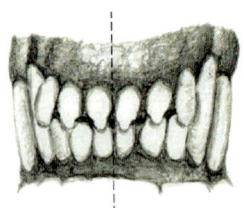

Notice the midline of the upper and lower jaws are aligned.

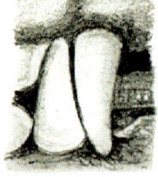

Normally, the lower canine should intersect the upper lateral incisor and upper canine.

Bite

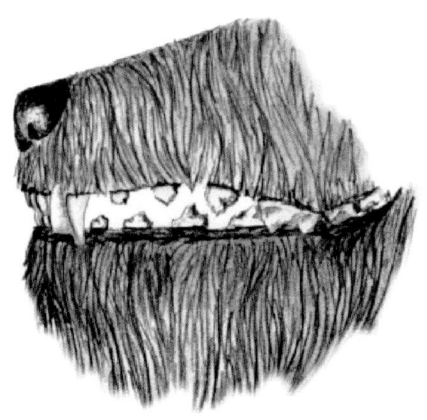

✓ Correct Scissor Bite

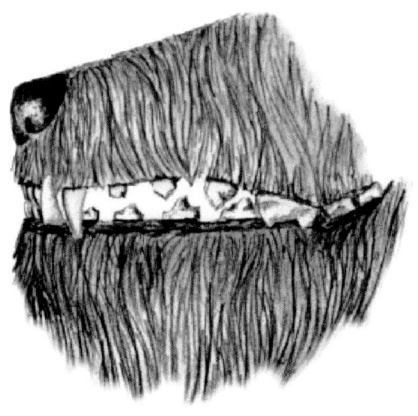

✗ Incorrect - Level Bite

✗ Incorrect - Overshot

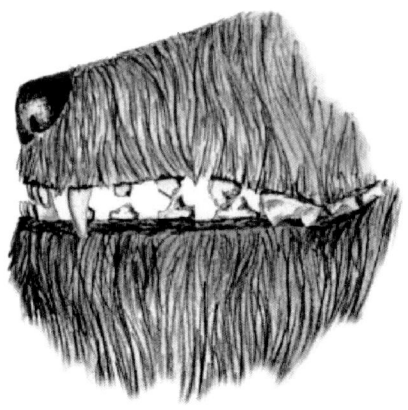

✗ Incorrect - Undershot

Head

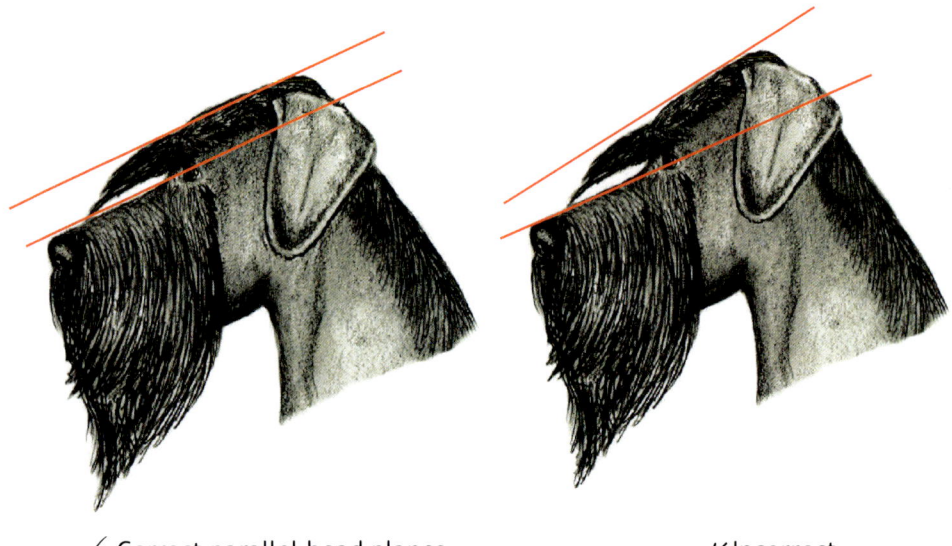

✓ Correct parallel head planes ✗ Incorrect

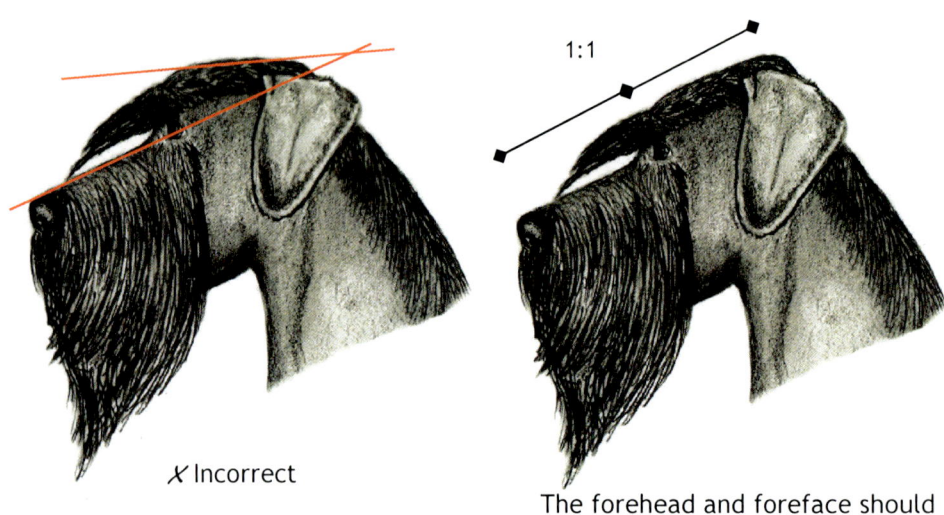

✗ Incorrect

1:1

The forehead and foreface should be of equal lengths, divided centrally by the stop.

✓ Correct - The head should be brick shaped, narrowing from the ears to the eyes and then gradually toward the end of the nose, ending in a blunt wedge.

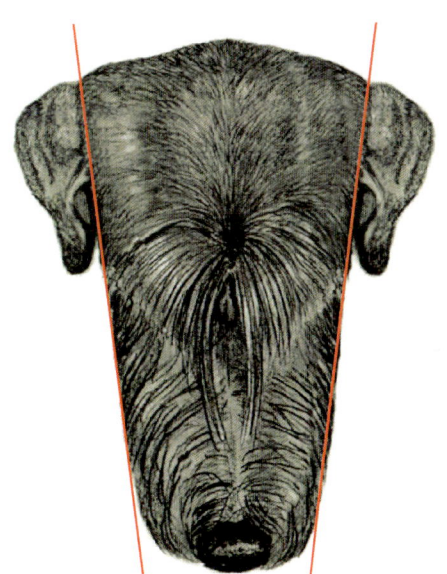

✗ Incorrect
Skull wide with narrow muzzle

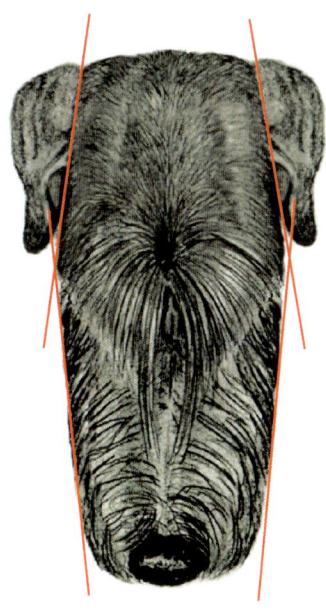

✗ Incorrect
Narrow skull, wide at cheeks with narrow muzzle

Shoulders

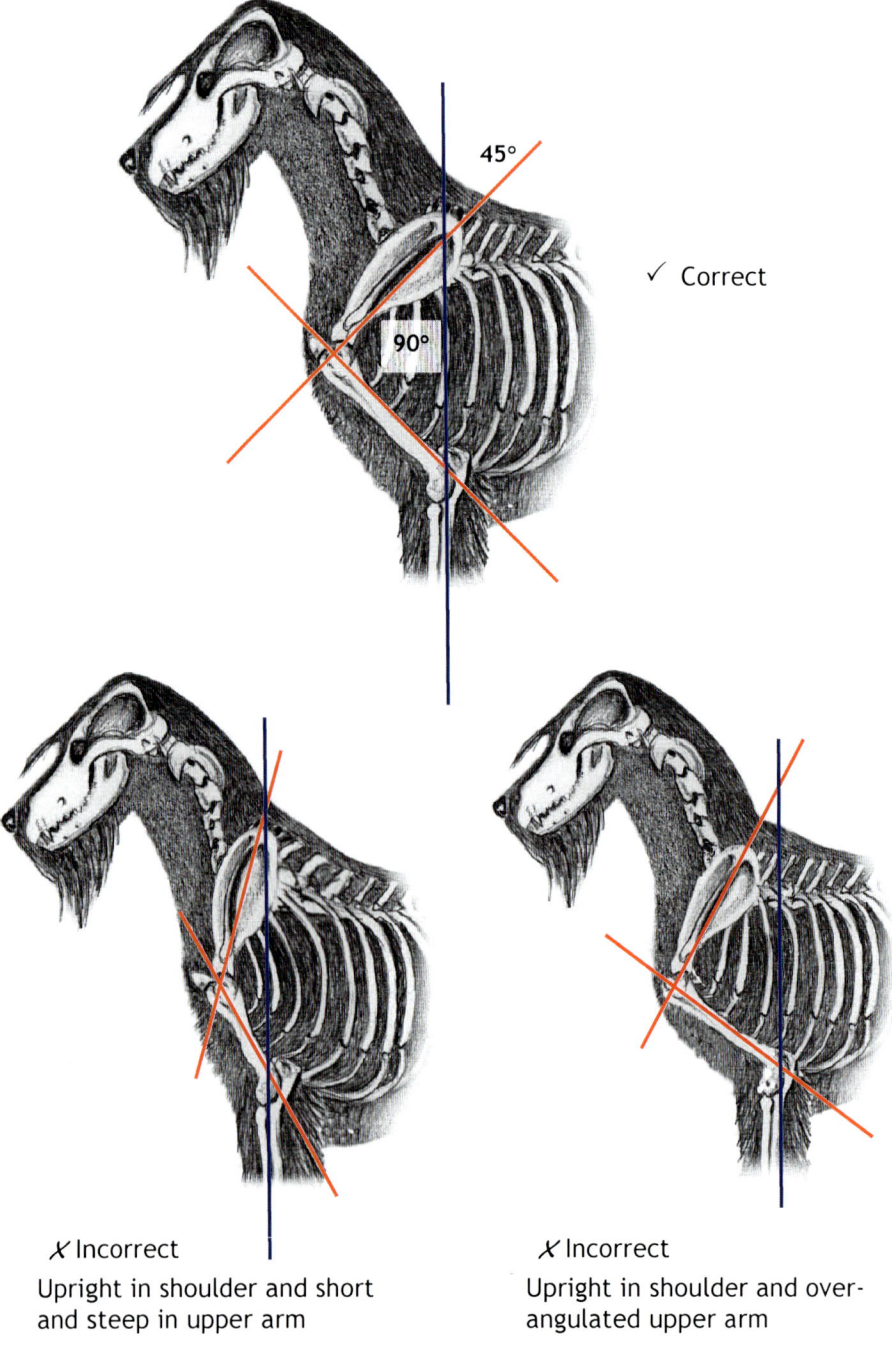

14

Neck

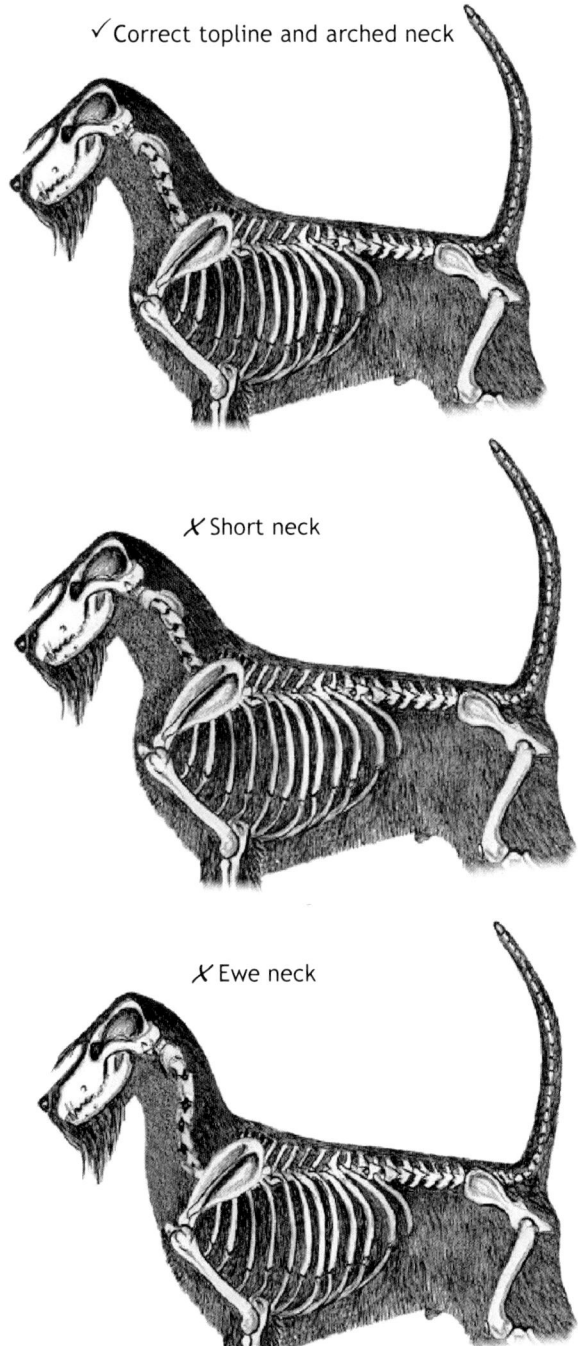

✓ Correct topline and arched neck

✗ Short neck

✗ Ewe neck

Topline and Tailset

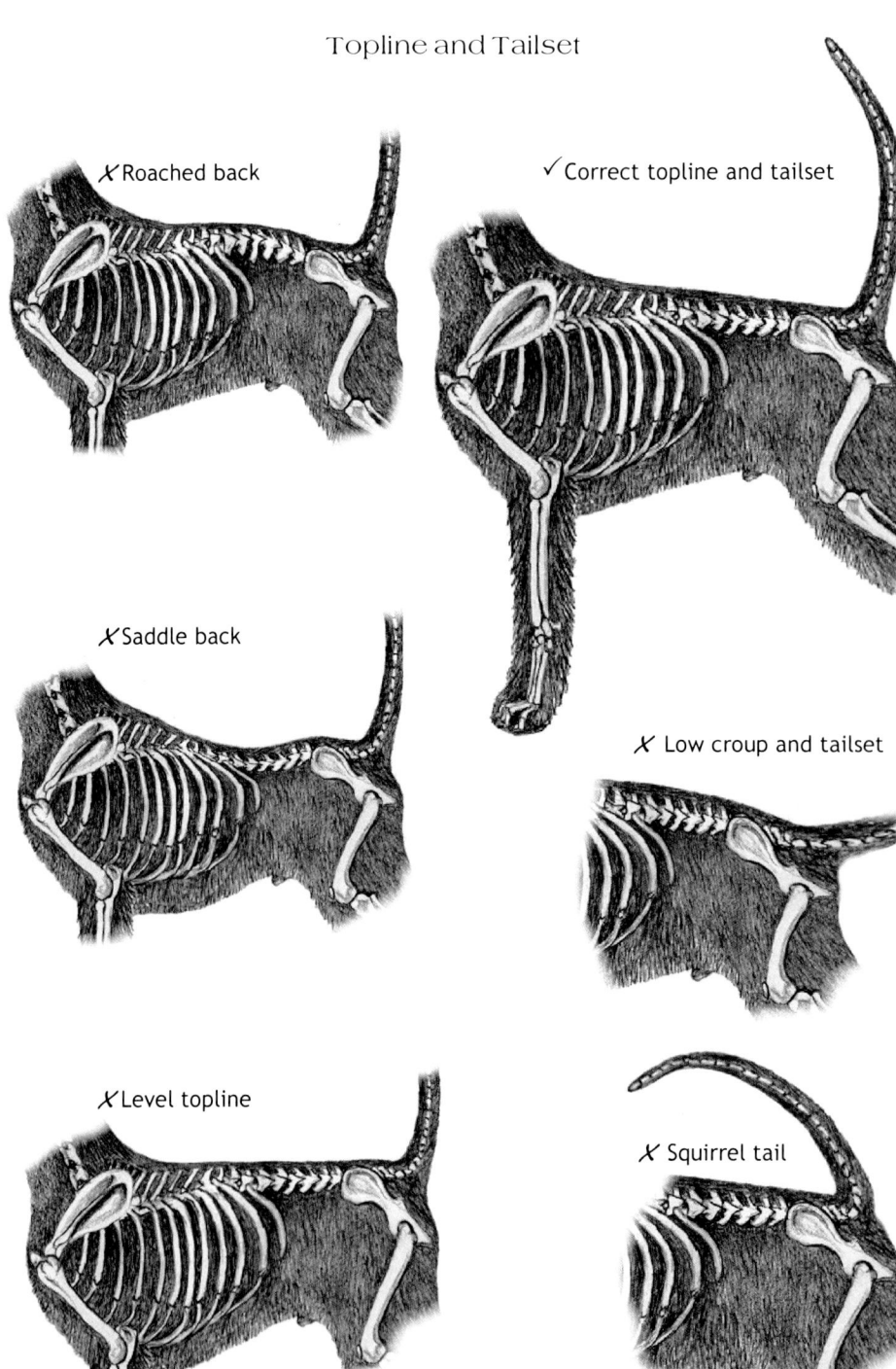

Movement

✓ Correct - good reach in front and driving behind

✗ Short steps front and back

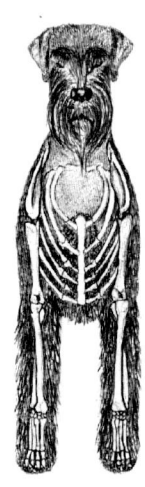 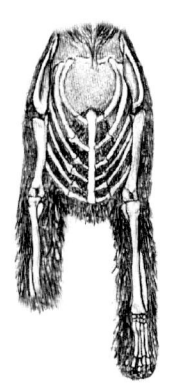

✓ Correct

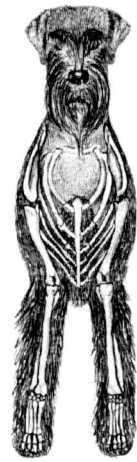 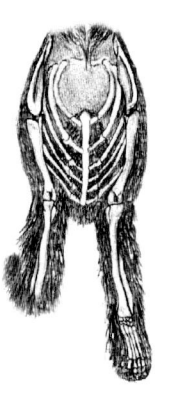

✗ Too narrow at the elbow

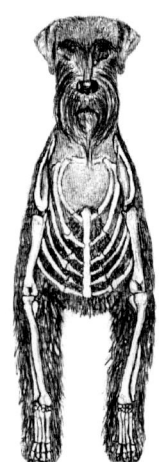 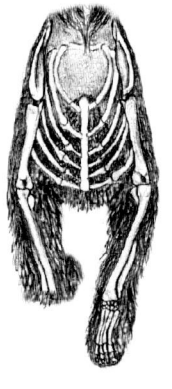

✗ Too wide at the elbow

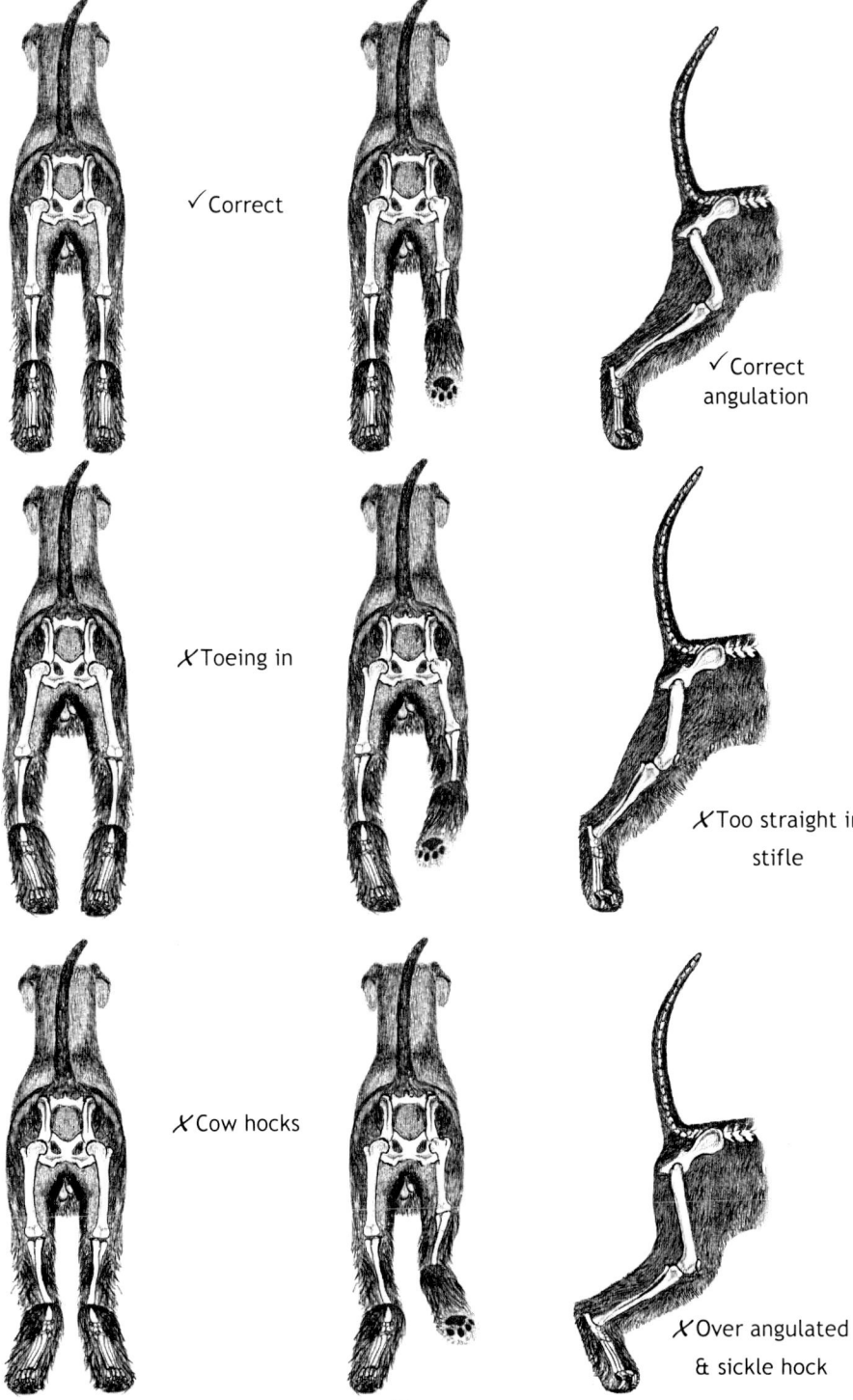

History of the Giant Schnauzer

The true origin of the Giant Schnauzer is somewhat uncertain; books from the 1830's speak of a wirehaired, strong and impressive dog resembling a larger version of the wirehaired pinscher. These dogs lived in the Bavarian Highlands of Southern Germany, and were therefore known as oberlanders, "highlanders".

Around the early 1800's oberlanders worked in extreme weathers, guarding and protecting farms, and driving pig and cattle herds to and from the meadows and markets. Their identity evolved, and was maintained, by a process of natural selection, the consequence of a tough and isolated existence.

Western Russian tribes had previously migrated from the Russian-Finland borders and settled in Southern Germany along with their Aftscharka "herdsman's" dogs. The Aftscharka were of differing sizes, colours and coat textures. They are thought to have been one of the ancestors of the oberlanders. However there is no conclusive evidence regarding the true origin of the oberlander.

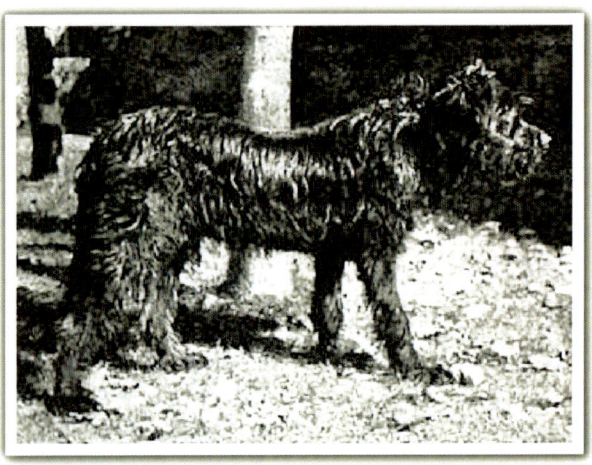

Russian herdsman's dog 'Aftscharka'

1850 Portrait of Princess Elizabeth of Bavaria, born in Munich, with her oberlander 'Shadow' by Emil Rabending

Towards the later 1800's dog fanciers in Munich took an interest in the oberlanders. Those bred in Munich at that time were known as Russen Schnauzer, Bierschnauzer (Beer Schnauzer), Bear Schnauzer or Munchener Schnauzer (Munich Schnauzer). These dogs were not only used for herding cattle but they also began to be used as watchdogs in Munich to protect breweries and butchers shops and to escort horse-drawn carts loaded with beer barrels.

The original oberlanders were crossed with oversized pepper and salt Standard Schnauzers, to obtain uniformity in the larger Schnauzer type. The oberlanders offered their size and power, and the standard Schnauzers contributed their harsh weather proof coat along with their vermin killing, droving and watchful instincts. Many of the first Giant Schnauzers were either pepper & salt or black, however grey-yellow and brown-yellow puppies were seen.

The first Schnauzer Club was founded in December 1907 by Dr Zurhellen in Munich; the Bavarian Schnauzer Club. The introduction of the first breed standard followed, based upon the same standard as the Pinscher. In October 1909 the Bavarian Schnauzer Club held a speciality show with dogs officially entered as Giant Schnauzers. This formally marked acceptance of the Giant Schnauzer as a recognised breed. However, the type, size, coat texture and colour of the entries varied greatly. The Judge found a black male, Bitru v. Weinberg, to be the best representative of the breed. Bitru became one of the important dogs in the original selective breeding of the Giant Schnauzer.

The first litter officially registered as the Munich Schnauzer was whelped in 1910. According to Gallant (1996) the litter was sired by a Pepper and Salt Giant Schnauzer; Ch Roland Rolandsheim. However other resources document that Roland Rolandsheim was himself a sibling from this first registered litter in 1910. Nevertheless he is an example of one of the first recorded Giant Schnauzers. Although short in stature, only 21¾ inches to the withers, he was a good example of the breed. Unfortunately as a stud dog his litters were inconsistent, and his career as a stud dog was therefore short-lived.

Ch Roland Rolandsheim

The initial development of the Giant Schnauzers was somewhat hindered by inconsistency, lack of experienced dog breeders and the hardship of the First World War. However, another important and influential male worthy of a mention was bred by Karl Kluftinger, of the Wetterstein kennel in 1914. His outstanding black male, Bazi v Wetterstein, became one of the most successful sires of the time.

Bazi v Wetterstein (born 1914)

The necessity for herding dogs gradually began to decrease with advancements of the road and rail networks, however the all-round hard working temperament, robustness, and intelligence of the Giant Schnauzer along with their ability to work under instruction enabled them to adapt to police and security work. During the First World War they were also used as a military dog. A son of Bazi v Wetterstein went on to become the first Giant Schnauzer to be awarded a police dog working certificate.

Dr C Calaminus, an experienced breeder and owner of the von Kinzigtal kennel, used a process of selective oberlander breeding combined with line breeding of the Munich Schnauzer. It was thought he also incorporated three other breeds, the black Great Dane, oversized Standard Schnauzers and possibly the Bouvier

De Flanders, to achieve his success. Unfortunately, Dr Calaminus never disclosed his breeding program, adding further vagueness to the history of the Giant Schnauzer. His male Felz v Kinzigtal became another of the successful foundation dogs of the breed.

Felz v Kinzigtal (1924)

After World War I the Bavarian Schnauzer Klub amalgamated with the Pinscher Klub forming the Pinscher-Schnauzer Association, later known as the Pinscher-Schnauzer Klub (PSK) in 1921. In 1923 an elaboration of the Schnauzer breed standard provided the original breed standard for the Giant Schnauzer.

In 1925 the Giant Schnauzer gained recognition as a working dog in Germany which allowed them to compete in the German Schutzhund (protection dog) tests and working trials. And in 1936 Mr Irrgang's Giant Schnauzer Peter, won the German national championship working trial for all breeds, beating the elitist of all German working dogs.

During the 1920's and 1930's when Giant Schnauzers began their international infiltration, they were shipped to North America. Canada saw the first registered Giant Schnauzers in 1934. The US military included the Giant Schnauzer in their war dog program "K-9 Corps", which began during World War II. The Giant Schnauzer was chosen as one of a small number of breeds suitable to undergo military training. They began a rigid military routine, including socialisation to gunfire, military vehicles and gas masks. The basic training routines were followed by specialised training for sentry duty, scout and patrol, messenger delivery and mine detection.

Following the Second World War 1939-1945 the numbers of Giant Schnauzers diminished, almost becoming extinct. After the war many breeders had to start practically all over again.

It was not until the 1960's that Giant Schnauzer breeders acquired breeding stock in the UK. The first dogs imported for breeding were a male and a female from Sweden by Donald Becker. Although the origins of the Giant Schnauzer stem from Germany, the initial dogs imported into the UK were from Sweden, Holland, Denmark, Italy, America, Czechoslovakia, Norway, Finland, Canada, Switzerland and Belgium.

The following is the pedigree of Scholten Stainless Steele, the UK's first champion, which shows the earliest imported and UK bred Giant Schnauzers.

CH SCHOLTEN STAINLESS STEELE Pepper/Salt	DONDEAU STRATHCONAGLEN BIT (Born in quarantine) Black	EELCO V D REINKENHOF Black	NEGUS V BUCK Black	
			CHRISTINA V D REINKENHOF Black	
		ANCARA V D POPULERIEN (Imported in whelp from Holland) Black	BILL V SCHNEIDERSTEIN Black	
			CYNTHIA V D DREI HARTEN Black	
	SCHOLTEN SABLE QUEEN (The First UK bred litter whelped in 1968) Black	RIESENGARDENS KING OF PUSZTAMERGES (Swedish Import) Black	GROLL V D REUSENBURG Black	FALK V.D SCHWANENTAL
				ELFI V.D REUSENBURG
			RIESENGARDENS BOGEY Black	FIN CH RIESENHEIMS WOTAN
				FIN CH JETTA V.D THALSOLE
		DONDEAU MARIANNE (Born in quarantine) Black	RIESENGARDENS DON Black	FIN CH RIESENHEIMS WOTAN
				FIN CH JETTA V.D THALSOLE
			WIGSANDS ISLE (Imported in whelp) Black	FIN CH BENTO
				FIN CH SKALLORNS RINGA

The first two Giant Schnauzer litters to be bred in the UK were in 1968 and 1969 out of Mrs Angela Gwinnell's female Dondeau Marianne. Both litters were sired by Donald Becker's Swedish import, Riesengardens King of Pusztamerges. Dondeau Marianne was herself born in quarantine out of Donald Becker's imported female Wigsands Isle who had already been mated to Riesengardens Don before being imported into the UK. The first litter registered with the Kennel Club to be classified under "Giant Schnauzers" came in 1971 by Riesengardens King of Puzstamerges ex. Scholten Sable Lady. Two male puppies were registered; Strathconaglen Buchanneer & Strathconaglen Pirate born on 1 July 1970. Prior to July 1971 Giant Schnauzers were registered with the Kennel Club under 'any other variety'.

The Giant Schnauzer in Britain
By Clifford Derwent (1987)

It is possible, and indeed likely that many readers of this handbook may only recently have heard of a Giant Schnauzer although those who regularly attend the major dog shows will have seen them - and once seen never forgotten!

Although his smaller cousins have been in this country for quite a long time, only a few Giants came to these shores in the sixties and it was not until the mid-seventies that there were any in number.

The first thing that strikes you about this breed of dog is his impressive style, combining sheer beauty with a formidable presence. He stands over two feet at the shoulder, has a wiry coat in Black or Pepper and Salt with a profuse beard and eyebrows. At shows and at working or obedience he will be as alive as a coiled spring. At home he is the most affectionate dog I know. However, before you rush off to buy your Giant I must warn you that certain things should be taken into account.

Firstly, he is not a giant dog, so if you want a big slow animal he is not for you. True, he weighs big at seven stone but that is about as heavy as a genuine working dog should be. So, in spite of his name, he is not a 'giant'. Nor is he naturally 'groomed to perfection'. He grows a lot of coarse coat which the Continentals strip off and which the Americans shampoo and blow dry (characteristically, we compromise between the two!).

Conny v. Inheidener See born 1968
Features in many of our pedigrees

Anyway something has to be done otherwise he soon becomes a matted hearthrug. He lives rather longer than most of his size, but takes a lot of time to grow up. Meanwhile he can be very boisterous if not downright wilful! He eats very well, but modern feeding practice makes it cheap to keep a dog well-fed today.

A real worry of our time is the bill from the vet, but as a breed the Giant is as fit as they come, and very hardy. I think that some of our dogs tend to dominate other dogs, but as a guard to hearth and home this breed should never disappoint.

He is not suitable (especially when young) to be left alone for long periods in a flat, and as a guard to a scrap metal yard he is frankly too bright not to lose all interest in the task. He really needs mental and physical activity and affection which he will return in full measure. Now, if you still want one, you will have to pay a good price. Whilst it is not invariably true that one only gets what one pays for in this life - nevertheless, it cannot be good sense to buy cheap when the dog will be around for more than a decade. But what you must not do is buy without care - and there lies the rub. It is my experience that some people give less thought to buying a dog than they would do to buying a second-hand car. Just think about it like that and you are half-way to safety - and sanity!

If you are still reading, then please allow me to give you a brief presentation of this truly majestic breed of your dog in our country. The correct name for the breed is actually 'Riesenschnauzer' which we have loosely translated to Giant Schnauzer.

The Schnauzer from whom he takes his name was, at the turn of the century, established as a sharp, medium-sized dog, aggressive as a killer of vermin and a hard watch-dog with a wiry coat of distinctive Pepper and Salt colour. He probably derived from a rough-haired Pincher (or German terrier). This latter name may well have come from the Saxon word 'pinch' and may have referred to grasping with the paws to hold before killing. The Schnauzer got his name from one particular dog exhibited in 1879 which presumably made an impression as a dog, but certainly the name indicating moustache or snout caught the imagination and stuck to the breed from that day on.

Long before 1879 however, way back into the romantic mists of time, there had been large coarse-coated dogs of colours ranging through black to yellow and red on the farms in the valleys of the Alps known as Bavarian Wolfhounds. A powerful dog of a size, strength and courage to keep and protect cattle herds and to survive in extremes of climate. At the turn of the 20th Century a number of breeders in the Munich area crossed over-large Schnauzers with these magnificent dogs. One can but hazard a guess of their intentions. Perhaps they wanted simply a grand Schnauzer, or to give class and style to the old Bavarian stock or, as I would believe, they wanted to create the perfect dog to fight not rats or wolves, but Man himself.

In 1909 the first Riesenschnauzer hit the world at a show in Munich. Naturally the colours varied from the traditional Schnauzer Pepper and Salt to pure and off-black. But what really caught the imagination was the arrival of an exciting new dog - smart, intelligent and formidable. Although a very great Pepper and Salt dog, Roland Rolandsheim, was whelped in 1910, the war years of 1914-18 curtailed any considerable development of these new dogs. At the end of the war however, there was another great black dog, Baxi v Wetterstein. The breed for that is what it had become, was taken up with enthusiasm by working people and because of its reputation came to the notice of the director of the State Training School. From 1918 to a climax in 1936 when the super dog Peter (trained in the State School) won the title of Reichs Seiger, the Riesenschnauzer reigned supreme as a working/guard dog and he surpassed the whole elite or working dogs.

1939 to 1945 were the second war years of tragedy for the Riesenschnauzer with the Pepper and Salt all but extinct. The immediate post-war years saw the explosion of the German Shepherd dog. This breed was taken up by the Americans who, by reason of their country's importance and wealth set it on the throne of working dogs. The sixties saw the arrival of the Dobermann (a relative of the Giant Schnauzer through the Pinscher, and in fact called a Pinscher until 1959), and later the Rottweiler.

Our breed's popularity grew much more slowly, possibly because he was one of a family group rather than an individual. But under the parental regulation and control of the Pinscher-Schnauzer- Klub since 1920 our breed's identity was re-established and popularity grew without loss of its characteristics.

Alfred Hohn, the author of 'Die Schnauzer and Pinscherrassen' says of the fifties and sixties "the breeding of performance qualities remained the goal of our idealistic people rearing working dogs". Nor was beauty overlooked as can be seen from the old pictures of progress from the beginning of the 1900's to 1970's. What I think is remarkable is the constant continuation of type throughout the years. Indeed, the picture of Carlo v Saidern whelped in 1925 shows an outline which would certainly win at any show in the world today.

The Schnauzer came to this country in the early '30s. He was joined later by his cousin the Miniature Schnauzer from Germany, but via America. In the sixties the Giant arrived and his welfare was taken over by the Schnauzer Club of Great Britain. The first breeder's dogs (as distinct from pet dogs) were introduced from Sweden by Donald Becker, a respected breeder and judge of the other two breeds. His bitch, Ilse, produced four puppies two of which were re-exported. Mr and Mrs Gwinnell had a bitch pup which was later mated to Mr Becker's other dog King. The other pup was mated to Schnauzers and the offspring were not recognised by our Kennel Club. Two other dogs played a part, Brutus v d Cleyburch and Kimbo av Ingehall, both Pepper and Salts.

From such a modest start came some good dogs, Strathconaglen Pirate of Burston, Scholten Sable Lady, Buchaneer and Odivane Marcus. Encouraged by the general interest Donald Becker and Sheila Gwynne-Williams imported Ancara, a Dutch bitch, in whelp. The star born was Mrs Gwinnell's Dondeau Strathconaglen Bit who sired the first dog and bitch breed Champions, Isara Diablo and Scholten Stainless Steel.

Ch. Isara Diablo
Imported - Champions in this country their progeny have influenced the breed

Unfortunately for the breed, Donald went off for a time to live in South Africa but he left behind his disciples in the form of Mesdames Moore, Gwinnell, Jefferys, Seed, Maher, Roberts and Williams - all ladies, except that I believe Mr Gwinnell was an influence behind the scenes.

Up to 1977 when the Kennel Club provided six sets of Challenge Certificates (three of which make a dog a Champion) the showing was limited and perhaps it is not surprising that one of the first C.C's was withheld through lack of quality. However, the amount of glory was soon to hand. In 1978 Mr Joe Braddon, the only judge qualified to award Kennel Club Challenge Certificates to every breed, made a Giant Schnauzer Best in Show at a general Championship show, the dog having won Groups under two famous international judges, Mrs de Casembroot and Mr Appleton. The dog, Ch Isara Diablo, was bred by Mrs Roberts (a German lady resident here) out of Mrs Moore's Odivane Modern Milly who later threw another Champion from another sire. Diablo was joined as a flagship for the breed by a Norwegian bitch Ch & Nor Ch Guldmandsbuktens Wenche of Nenevale, imported by Mrs Jenny Harrison-Smith. This outstanding bitch has influenced the Black dogs with her progeny more than any other to date. Space precludes mention of many other dogs of high quality, but the most influential Black sire so far is Ch Ambassador of Catalanta, born in quarantine from a bitch imported from the U.S.A. and piloted to success by Mrs Gill Saville. Other Champions have been brought here from the continent and elsewhere, even from behind the Iron Curtain, to improve our stock including German Ch Illo v Gunterstal, a Black and Int Ch Adonis vd Havenstad, a Pepper and Salt.

Nor & Eng Ch Guldmansbuktens Wenche
Her progeny have influenced the breed in this country more than any other to date

The latest import to come, see and conquer is Mrs Wilberg's Black, Rosapik Othello of Kanix who, scarcely out of puppyhood, won Best in Show against all breeds at Bournemouth Championship Show 1985. He along with other very worthy Champions will be chasing Diablo's record in the years to come, no doubt. Whilst it seems to be true that the Blacks are more eye-catching than the Pepper and Salts and have certainly gained more success at shows both here and abroad, the Pepper and Salt soon becomes an acquired taste. He is just as good a worker with the same grand temperament. Indeed, Mrs Radcliffe's Burston's Silver Avenger (bred by Mrs Seed) carries the enviable performance letters CD ex, UDex WDex after his name.

Clearly it is not possible to mention all the breeders who have made our success possible, nor to list all our great dogs. Indeed such a list would only bore the reader and this would be a pity for our breed is anything but boring. We now have our own Championship judges, our own breed club, influence at home and abroad, good friends and those who know dogs.

We are all here to help you share with us the joy and pride of owning a Giant Schnauzer.
So what, dear reader, are you waiting for?

The Giant Schnauzer in Britain
Update 1998

It is going to be a hard task to update Clifford Derwent's review of the breed in England since 1985, and I will only be mentioning those dogs who stand out in my memory.

Ch Ambassador of Catalanta produced several champion offspring, one of which was Ch Nenevale Bumper Bundle, CDex Udex. He himself produced Ch Nixador Black Saracen, Ch Parisgarden Delilah and Champion littermates Jannem Tarquin and Teshekkur, who did the double at Crufts.

The Finnish import Ch Rosapik Othello was a very consistent winner himself, and although he died at only three years old he proved to be a very dominant sire. His offspring included Ch Paris garden William, Ch Jannern Sadik, Ch Dicarl Black Panther and Ch Dicarl Black Adder. Also in the same litter were Ch Nenevale Yvonne, Ch Nenevale Yvette and Ch Nenevale Yesterdayman, who in his turn was used extensively at stud and produced many champions. Added to this, the Ch Rosapik Othello of Kanix daughters Ch Sandridge Guilietta and, last but not least, the outstanding Ch Sandridge Kirry, who, apart from winning a string of C.C.'s, distinguished herself as a brood bitch, becoming 1991 top Giant Brood Bitch, runner-up Working Group, sixth top Brood All Breeds and 1993 top Brood Bitch. She was exported to Sweden in whelp to Shinda v.d. Noorderenk at Nixador, where she produced even more winners.

Ch Xeros v Buck of Nenevale

Newer imports included Ch Xeros v Buck of Nenevale from Germany. He is the winner of 24 C.C.'s, numerous Best of Breed awards, including Club Best in Show wins, and has sired five champions.

Another more recent import is Ch Stablemasters Ex Lee from Finland. He won five C.C's, and Best of Breeds in five consecutive shows. How important his progeny will be lies still in the future.

Ch Stablemasters Ex Lee

American import Skansens Quality at Zantana stayed in England for six months after quarantine, leaving behind three champion offspring, whose influence will be seen through their progeny.

The Giant Schnauzer in Britain
Update 2010 By Kirk Moss

The last update finished by mentioning the three champion offspring of Skansens Quality at Zantana, Jannem Mumterem and the litter mates, Jafrak Keep Cool and Jafrak Keep Talking. Keep talking was a very successful show girl winning 19 CC's and holding the bitch CC record for several years.

Ch Jafrak Keep Talking

Ch Jafrak Keep Cool

Keep Cool was also very successful in the show ring and when mated to another American import, Skansens Quality at Jafrak, produced the very successful Ch. Jafrak California Dreamin. These three dogs together with the males Ch. Foxwood Double

CH Jafrak California Dreaming

CH Foxwood Double Edged

Edged, Ch. Jafrak See If I Care and Ch. Nenevale Landmaker were very dominant in the 90's.

CH Jafrak See If I Care

CH Nenevale Landmaker

Ch. Xeros v. Buck of Nenevale sired 5 champions, Foxwood Double Edged, Foxwood Double Entendre at Zanclus, Nenevale Front Runner, Nenevale Flower Power of Springflite and Nenevale Casanova of Lauril .
Four of those five went on to produce champions themselves.

Skansens Quality at Jafrak was mated to another American import, Skansens Tortellini at Jafrak, and produced three more champions, Jafrak Zucchini, Porcini and Dolcelata.

Zucchini was a producer of three champions, Jafrak Wheel of Fortune, Jafrak Dream On and Jafrak Dream Come True. Dolcelata produced a champion son, Jafrak Philippe Olivier, who will get a mention later.

Another import came in to the country from Spain around this time called Donjuan de Pichera at Foxwood. He was to have a big impact on the breed in the UK being used extensively. He produced seven champion offspring, Foxwood Incognito, Foxwood Business as Usual, Boujan Juan da Bra, Springflite out of the Blue, Indigo Chief Foxwood, Riesenheim Cebreros and Zamoranos Picasso.

Donjuan De Pichera At Foxwood

Picasso was the most successful of these, winning many CC's, groups and best in shows, but, by no means, did he have an easy ride. Many times he did battle with Ch. Foxwood Incognito and Ch. Nenevale Quip Modest, regularly sharing the top awards.

Other big winning females of the time were Ch. Ingella Fancy Dancing of Nenevale and Ch. Stablemaster's Seventh Heaven of Leebay, who was imported from Finland being a litter sister to the very influential stud dogs Ch. Stablemaster's Superman and Superplay.

Picasso produced two champions. When mated to Jafrak California Dreamin he produced Ch. Jafrak Brushstrokes who is the current bitch CC record holder with 25 CC's.

CH Jafrak Brushstrokes
The current bitch CC record holder

He also sired Ch. Bellgard Paloma Picasso who has a champion grand daughter Ch. Bellgard Ghetto Stiletto.

Ch Bellgard Paloma Picasso

Ch Bellgard Ghetto Stiletto at Philoma

Picasso also had a litter brother, Zamoranos Dali that produced a champion daughter, Ch. Ferncliffe's Bete Noire, who regularly battled hard in the show ring with Brushstrokes, making it a very exciting time.

Another of the Donjuan sons, Ch. Riesenheim Cebreros, was mated to the Donjuan daughter, Ch. Foxwood Business as Usual, and, together, they produced Ch. Inka Hoots from Foxwood who was mated to Ch. Riesenheim Suited n' Booted for Daleiden (himself a Cebreros grandson) and went on to produce two champions Ch. Draxpark Big Shot and Ch. Draxpark Hot Shot.

We must now go back a couple of years, to when Picasso was Top Giant 2000, 2001 and 2002. In 2003 a new young male emerged to challenge Picasso's reign. This male was Ch. Jafrak Philippe Olivier. He was sired by world winner Luther King du Bujol by Ch. Jafrak Dolcelata, herself a group winner.

Dolcelata had been taken to France, under the new pet passport scheme, by her breeders, Jack & Francis Krall. Philippe was kept from the subsequent litter by Dolcelata's owners, Kevin & Sandie Cullen.

CH Jafrak Philippe Olivier

Philippe had an outstanding show career, was top giant 2003, 2004 and 2005 winning countless groups 42 CC's and 14 all breed Best In Show culminating in Best in Show Crufts 2008 -the ultimate achievement.

While Philippe had a relatively limited stud career, he did, however, produce four champions. They were the litter sisters Jafrak Philadelphia (who was mated to Ch.Riesenheim Capt. Fantastic to produce the Top Giant 2009, Ch.Jafrak Le Fantasie) and Jafrak Philharmonica. Also, the litter mates Riesenheim Versace and Riesenheim Suited n' Booted for Daleiden.

CH Jafrak Dolcelata

In 2005 Suited n' Booted won B.I.S at the Giant Schnauzer Club Championship Show, beating his father, Philippe, for the first time, and so taking up the gauntlet to challenge for the title of Top Giant.

Suited n' Booted went on to win 33 CC's, several group wins and over 20 group placings. He was Top Giant 2006, 2007 and 2008, like the dogs before him, he has also gone on to produce Champion offspring.

CH Riesenheim Suited N'Booted for Daleiden

His first son, Ch. Draxpark Big Shot, was the breed's first tailed champion after the docking of tails became illegal in April 2007. And his sister Ch. Draxpark Hot Shot became the breed's first female tailed champion in July 2010.

Litter brother and sister CH Draxpark Big Shot & CH Draxpark Hot Shot
The first UK dog and bitch tailed champions

CH Riesenheim Bite the Bullet

His other champion son, Riesenheim Bite the Bullet was top male 2009 and is in the lead for Top Giant 2010.

Suited n'Booted's litter brother, Riesenheim Galliano, also produced two champion offspring, Ch. Foxwood Xtravaganza and Ch. Foxwood Indesputable at Barnsdale.

CH Foxwood Xtravaganza

CH Foxwood Indesputable At Barnsdale

Other dogs that are worthy of note are Ch. Bowenhurst Silver Boss. He is the only pepper and salt to achieve his champion status in the last decade.

CH Bowenhurst Silver Boss

Also, the trio from the Primavista kennel, bred by Mike Whitney & Antonio Di Martino. Champions Sofia Loren, Rumba Carumba, and Mambo Italiano, all from the same litter sired by Craggyknowe Cheeky Chico at Primavista by Bellgard Marie Antoinette at Primavista.

CH Primavista Sofia Loren

CH Primavista Rumba Carumba

CH Primavista Mambo Italiano

In recent times we have had an influx of Russian bred dogs. Firstly, Skansens Yankee Clipper at Jafrak. Although he came from the US he is Russian sired.

He has produced two champion children so far, Ch Habarny Yankee Giggles and Ch. Jafrak Causing A Commotion. He also has two champion grandchildren, Ch Khinjan Cinnabar and Ch. Grovelea Foxtrot.

Skansen's Yankee Clipper at Jafrak

Dgentli Bon Molotov at Foxwood has a champion daughter in Foxwood Bombshell.

FCI Int.Ch.Savali Level Hi-If at Ferncliffe came into this country from the Ukraine (via Iceland) at 5 years old and won a CC and several RCC's, before retiring to stud. Also, a nephew of Svali's, Con Amore Da Felmor To Coldnose, was imported from Italy, gaining two CC's. Both of these dogs' offspring are now entering the show ring and you will have to wait for the next update to find out if, and how, these, and other stud dogs, have influenced the breed.

FCI INT CH Savali Level Hi-Fi At Ferncliffe (IMP UKR)

Con Amore Da Felmor To Coldnose (IMP ITA)

The Pepper and Salt Giant Schnauzer in Britain
By A Gwinnell (1987)

The Pepper and Salt Giants made their appearance in the U.K. about eight years later than the Blacks, very few have been imported so the development has been much slower, though not without its successes.

The first import, from Holland, was Brutus van de Cleyburch brought in by Mrs Mary Moore (Odivane). He was by Dutch Ch Akim van de Cleyburch ex Ondra van Widderhof, a father/daughter mating, though both were Pepper and Salt, the background breeding was a combination of Pepper and Salt and Black. The Widderhof Kennel were the top Pepper and Salt producers from 1956 until the early 1970's when they faded out. Brutus was mated to Blacks, and his daughters put back to him, this produced a fair proportion of Pepper and Salt, though at the time they were considered to be rather on the small side. It is only with a greater familiarity of this colour and its background is it realised that the majority of Pepper and Salts across all bloodlines are smaller than Blacks. They are of course completely within the Standard.

The second Pepper and Salt to appear in 1973 was not an import but produced from two Blacks, the import Dondau Strathconaglen Bit and Scholten Stable Queen, Mrs Angela Gwinnell was the owner/breeder. This was Scholten Stainless Steel, a bitch, who, when C.C's were offered in 1977 became the breed's first Champion, and up to this time the only Pepper and Salt one. The third member of the trio was Kimbo av Ingehall, imported as a pet and fortunately acquired by Mrs Chris Williams, Penbari Standards, who then passed him to Mrs Fio Roberts, (Isara). He was by Marko v.d. Lorquelle ex Kinnie Av Ingehall, yet another Pepper and Salt with Black breeding in the background as Kinnie was a granddaughter of Riesengardens Ano, a brother of Riesengardens Don and Riesengardens Bogey, the grandparents of Scholten Stable Queen. It is interesting to note than Eisa Westlaufer (Widderhof) tried very hard to incorporate this bitch into her breeding programme, but Kinnie never produced to a Widderhof male.

These three Pepper and Salts formed the basis of the British breeding. Although Brutus sired two Black C.C. winners, his grandchildren are of more importance.

Stainless Steel mated to Kimbo produced Scholten Merchant of Menace and Scholten Nickel of Nixador (three R.C.C's) Mrs Thea Jeffery's Pepper and Salt foundation bitch. To her son Menace, she produced Scholten Steel Merchant. Her third litter was to Musoneri Black Aragonite, Brutus' winning son which produced Scholten Faintly Saintly and Scholten Driftwood of Kiznic, Mrs Nicky Simpson's first Giant. The final winner, producer, was Proud Pepper of Swarbrick (I.R.C.C.) a Brutus grand-daughter, by Kimbo, owned by Mrs Mary Seed, Burston. These few Giants in various combinations formed the background of the British side of the current stock.

Although no particularly outstanding Giants were bred in the period of 1979/84 due to the lack of new blood, several bitches were produced that proved to be key factors when it finally did arrive in 1979. Mrs Seed mated Proud Pepper to Steel Merchant to breed her first litter and exported a bitch, Burstons Silver April, to Mr Cyriel de Meulenear in Belgium, there, mated to his outstanding dog, Ch Adonis v.d. Havenstad, April produced his successor, the equally outstanding Ch Faust v.d. Havenstad.

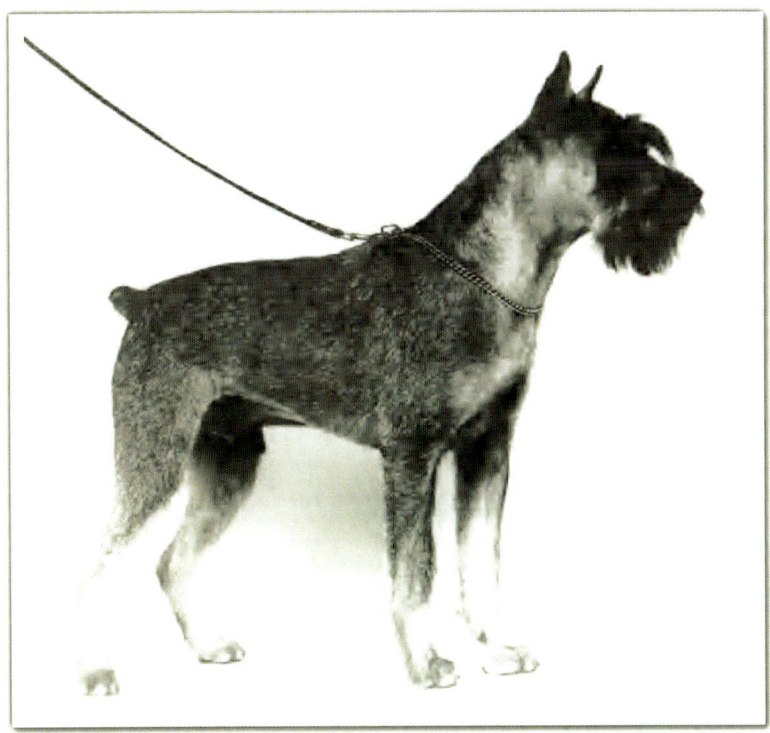

CH Adonis vd Havenstad

Faust with Sylvia Hammastrom

CH Faust vd Havenstad

Photos courtesy of Mrs Sylvia Hammastrom

With the result Mr de Meulenear lent Adonis to Mesdames Jefferys and Gwinnell. He combined very well with the British stock, in particular Kiznic Kalpyso bred by Mrs Simpson from Driftwood and Burstons Silver Aglow of Kiznic. A bitch from her first litter, sent to Italy has won top honours in Italy, Germany and Austria, this is Magic Star of Nixador exported by Mrs Jefferys. Also, in the ownership of Mrs Diane Hounslow, Rillaton, Kalypso produced a second litter containing several good males who were winning well in competition here with the Blacks. Mrs Jefferys also bred two winning dogs Nixador the Consul and Nixador the Diplomat of Darford from Adonis and Scholten Phantom Lady.

This is the state of the Pepper and Salt at present, we still need further new stock to be used as widely and wisely as possible, so that we do not have to resort to using Black as an outcross. Although our lines have incorporated Black in the past it is not an easy decision to take as Black is dominant and does mask other colours a dog may be carrying. The most unfortunate colour is red or tan, as a red Pepper and Salt is quite useless, it cannot be shown and should never be bred from, the occasional Pepper and Salt that appears in a Black litter is a practical addition, on the Black angle, if puppies from a colour cross mating are bred back into Black lines it is possible to introduce a dilution factor to the detriment of pure Black. So great care must be taken and not done lightly as just an experiment.

The Pepper and Salt Giant
Update By A Gwinnell (1998)

The progress of the Pepper and Salt Giant Schnauzer is still very slow in comparison with the Blacks at exhibition level. Although many more are bred now than in the past, very few are shown. One reason is that three of the original Pepper and Salt Kennels who bred and showed have given up, or greatly restricted all activities. Mrs Simpson, Kiznic, gave up in 1985. Mrs Seed, Burston, has also reduced her programme and Mrs Gwinnell had to cut all breeding and showing in 1989 for personal reasons and has not yet restarted. However, the Late Mrs Thea Jeffery's, Nixador, and Mrs Di Hounslow, Rillaton, kept the flag flying.

The arrival of Ch Adonis v.d. Havenstad in 1984 gave a much needed boost as he was the most important and widely used import. Even so, there have only been six C.C. and R.C.C. winners in the past ten years, though a great bonus is that two of these became Champions. A few others have made it into the Stud Book, but left no mark.

The first two winning Adonis sons were bred by Thea Jefferys in 1984 out of the bitch, Scholten Phantom Lady, loaned to her by Mrs Angela Gwinnell. Sadly, a repeat mating, when returned to her breeder resulted in only one puppy dog. Nixador the Consul was retained by Mrs Jefferys, while Nixador the Diplomat went to Mr Terry Radford, who campaigned him very successfully for several years. Unfortunately he left no get.

Mrs Di Hounslow followed in January 1985 with Rillaton Misty Shadow by Adonis out of Kiznic Kalypso, owned and shown by Mr Peter Key. Misty Shadow was made up in 1987 to become the first male Pepper and Salt Champion. His major triumph was Best in Show at the Giant Schnauzer Club Ch show that year. Mrs Hounslow then used Nixador The Consul on Kalypso in 1987, resulting in two more winning males, Rillaton Misty Mountain Man and Mrs Jefferys Rillaton Misty Chief at Nixador.

Rillaton Misty Mountain Man

The most recent and most outstanding Pepper and Salt is the bitch Ch Isara Quella at Nixador, by Rillaton Misty Chief at Nixador out of a bitch of Mrs Fio Roberts breeding, Isara Minerva. To date she has won four C.C.'s, three Best of Breed, and four R.C.C's, Best in show at The Schnauzer Club of Great Britain Ch Show in 1993, and Best in Show at The giant Schnauzer Club Ch show in 1995. Her breeding is interesting as she is very closely bred on the three original Pepper and Salts with seven lines to Ch Scholten Stainless Steel and five lines each to Brutus v.d. Cleyburch from Ovidane and Kimbo av Ingeall and only one line to Adonis in six generations, which turns in almost a full circle to 1984 when once again there is a very real need for new bloodlines.

Meanwhile, Mrs Jefferys exported successfully to several countries, resulting in overseas Nixador Champions.

The Pepper and Salt Giant
Update 2010 By P Wollen & A Gwinnell

In the early 90s Diane imported Stablemaster's Ex Lee (Esko) to improve the quality of the pepper and salts for her next generation. Esko was mated to Ch. Isara Quella at Nixador to produce Nixador Van Artist at Rillaton, who, put to Rillaton Manakin produced Rillaton Painted Lady, an exceptional example of the breed who achieved 1CC.

After the passing of Thea Jefferies in 1997, Diane continued as the main Pepper and Salt Giant Schnauzer breeder in the UK. Diane's Rillaton stock have been exported to a number of European countries and are behind many champions, renown for their good bone and heads, with strong fore chest, correct coat, good temperaments, and being extremely good movers.

Giant Schnauzer Club Championship Show 19th Oct 2003

Diane Hounslow winning the progeny class; sired by Rillaton Misty Mountain Lad.

From left to right Bowenhurst Just One Look, Bowenhurst Silver Boss, Rillaton Misty Mountain Lad, Bowenhurst Intuition, Rillaton Ivory Dreaming Las, and Rillaton Priceless Pepper handled by Diane.

In 1998 Penny Wollen had her first litter using Nixador Van Artist with Rillaton (a black dog carrying pepper and salt) to Nixador Magic Hula daughter of Ch Isara Quella. One of the progeny Bowenhurst Silver Robin received a Reserve CC at Crufts 2001. This litter produced 6 black and 4 pepper and salts, only 1 pepper and salt bitch, not a good enough colour to breed from, so she bought in from Robert Joy, Bellgards Ivory Teardrops. In 2003 put to Di Hounslow's Rillaton Misty Mountain Lad produced Ch Bowenhurst Silver Boss and his sister Bowenhurst Intuition, who won 2 Reserve CC's.

CH Bowenhurst Silver Boss

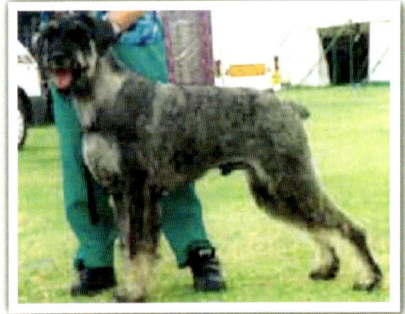

Rillaton Misty Mountain Lad

During 2004 Diane joined forces with Alexandra Van De Honert, the Winriks Hof kennel from the Netherlands, bringing in new blood lines to the Rillaton stock. Diane, accompanied by her two close friends Jean Broxson and Ray Sanderson, made a few epic journeys via motor-home to bring the new dogs into the country.

In 2005 Diane also bred Rillaton Winrik Popstar at Riesenheim, sired by CH Phaidon v Winriks Hof out of Rillaton Ivory Starlet. Winrik Popstar owned by Mr Ray Sanderson and known as 'Elvis' is currently one of the only Pepper and Salt Giant Schnauzers being campaigned in the show ring today. So far he has gained 1 CC and 2 Reserve CCs. Unfortunately Diane was diagnosed with cancer in 2008, and continuing her devotion to the breed, she admirably judged Giant Schnauzers at the National Working & Pastoral Breeds Championship Show in June 2009. Sadly Diane lost her battle with the disease in August 2009.

Diane's husband Richard is hoping to continue the Rillaton affix on a small scale.

Rillaton Winrik Popstar at Riesenheim winning the dog CC at SKC 2008

Skansen's Koira of Kelcanrick

A consistent pepper and salt show person since 1998 is Rosemary Rickard, firstly with Nixador and Rillaton stock, latterly importing Skansens from America. Showing not only in the UK but also Europe. Nixador Merely Magical (litter sister to Nixador Magic Hula) won 1cc and 2 Reserve cc's. Skansens Koira of Kelcanick (4 CACIB's & 4 BOB). Kelcanick Rhosyn Mair (progeny of Koira) 7 CACIB, 1 Res, 4 BOB. Skansens Koda of Kelcanrick 5 CACIB, 1 Res. 1 BOB.

The crossing of the two colours is only allowed in USA and UK, this making the gene pool in Europe quite small. Because of the clever colour crossings produced in the UK, British stock is now of an interest to European and breeders worldwide.

Robert Joy, who was greatly influenced by Diane, having worked at her kennels as a lad, went on to establish his own Bellgard kennels in 1980, consisting of black and pepper and salt lines, going back to Nixador and Rillaton. In 1995 Rob acquired his first pepper and salt bitch from the late Thea Jefferies, Nixador Magic Cinders, who was a granddaughter of the famous Ch.Isara Quella at Nixador (bred by Mrs Roberts). From her first litter came Bellgard Ivory Zambia, who sired Bellgard's Ivory Teardrops, who, in turn, was the dam of Bowenhurst Silver Boss.

Recently, a litter has been produced by Silver Boss to Bellgard's Ghetto Glitter. Although this produced a black litter, with pepper and salt behind it, the new bloodlines will be useful in generations to come. A promising dog and bitch have been retained for this purpose.

Ch Isara Quella

The Working Giant Schnauzer
(Fit for purpose, fit for life)
By Mark Tyson Home Office Police Dog Instructor (retired)

In the early 1800's the first mention of dogs in Germany used for working from the Pinscher group of dogs were dogs like the Rattenfanger, a small dog used on farms to kill vermin. Or the Saubeller or Saufinder. Sau is the Germany term for pig or boar. Beller means barker, and finder as the same significance in English as in German.

These dogs were found over the Southern German Hinterland (Wurttemberg, Swabia and Bavaria) were strong enough to herd pigs and cattle on farms and even to be used in driving wild boar.

This type of large dog was hidden on isolated farms of the Bavarian Highlands and has therefore been known as Oberlander. We know nothing for certain about the Oberlanders origin. It might go back to the Mollossian dogs imported by the Romans 2000 years ago. We know that these dogs were used on the large farms and were all rounder's. Guarding the premises was almost certainly his most important duty.

Around the turn of the Century Munich dog fanciers obtained a number of Oberlander dogs and Munich became the breeds second home, thus giving rise to the name Munchen Schnauzer (Munich Schnauzer). The alternative name Bier Schnauzer (Beer Schnauzer) was taken from the fact that these dogs were often used by the breweries to escort the delivery of the dray.

Prior to the First World War two elements came together. The Oberlander carried a tradition of all round work dog on and around the farm. Most of the time he was under mans control and had to follow instructions, but he also at times had to work on his own and show initiative and make up his own mind, over the years an environment that forged a reliable and active dog. To these basic qualities add some Schnauzer/Pincher qualities and the result could only be a fierce dog, keen to work for a handler who was a leader, otherwise this dog would take the initiative.

The First World War saw these type of dogs come to prominence, used as messenger dogs, tracking, guarding and attack dogs to name but a few of many uses. The vanishing flocks and the fact that cattle were no longer driven to markets released a number of Shepherd and Cattle dogs from their ancestral jobs, such as the German Shepherd Dog, Rottweiler and Giant Schnauzer. Owing to centuries of selected breeding for hard work these dogs were with adequate training perfectly suitable to undergo a transition to Police work. The first

Giant Schnauzer to obtain the Polizei Hund (PH Police Dog) working certificate was Helfried V. Schnonau around 1918.

In the early 1920's the leading kennel organisations worked out rules and regulations for tests and competition for dogs. The Germans called there programme Schutzhund (Protection Dog) this consists of Tracking, Obedience and Protection Work with three different levels of difficulty. In order to be allowed to participate in these tests and working trials each parent breed club had to apply to the German Kennel Club for recognition of their breed as a Gebrauchshund loosely translated Utility Dog which created some confusion in some Countries with a Utility Group. A more accurate translation of Gebrauchshund (or its German synonym diensthund) is a dog to be used by and to serve man – that means an active working dog to be classified in The Working Group.

In the early 1920's because of the popularization of the Gebrauchshund in Germany, several government training centres were established including one in Grunheide under the management of Colonel Schonherr, a Giant Schnauzer enthusiast and member of the Pinscher/Schnauzer Klub.

A steady progression of working dogs followed from 1927 the German Pinscher/Schnauzer Klub organised annually The Bundesleistungsiegerprufung (Nation Championship Working Trials) for Giant Schnauzer's. Only the twenty best Giants selected were allowed to participate.

On the 1 January 1937 the working dog class was introduced in Breed Shows in the FCI affiliated Countries. This class is reserved for dogs belonging to a recognised Working Breed and which previously have obtained a recognised working certificate such as SCH 1 (Schutzhund) or IPO 1 (Internationale Prufungsordnung) this measure was taken to simulate working fans to show their dogs and at the same time to simulate the breed ring fans to work their dogs. In other words to promote the idea of beauty and brains.

In 1938 there were over seven hundred Giants being shown in Germany. The Second World War, because of food shortages, not only curtailed the breeding of Giant Schnauzers, but that of all large dogs. The Germans were back to square one, but have succeeded in replenishing the gene pool and around fifty Giants per month succeed in working tests today.

In conclusion it is not only my opinion but a logical conclusion that the aim of the creators and the work of the promoters, that is the parent breed club in the Country of origin must be respected and adhered to. Every breeder has of course the duty to improve the breed and to bring the progeny as close as possible to the breed standard and not to change the breed standard so as to affect the working capabilities of the breed. It is a fact that outside his native Country the Giant Schnauzer is not considered a Police Dog or worked as such.

Why must there be a German Giant Schnauzer, a Spanish type, a British type, a breed ring type or working type? Why not one type a Giant Schnauzer with brains who is put together in such a way that enables him the best possible way to perform the work for which he was developed. Don't ignore the brains and change the exterior to such an extent that they diminish the working capacity that is the natural heritage of the breed.

In 1959 Werner Jung formulated the breeding aims for the Giant Schnauzer as follows: - "Nobility – Beauty – Performance". In the PSK Jubilee edition Peter Butzik added Health and surrounding friendliness. With health emphasising the breeder's duty to eradicate hereditary diseases such has Hip Dysplasia. Surrounding friendliness is an essential of any well adjusted working dog. Nobility and Beauty should be expected from any pure bred dog. Performance undoubtedly reflects on working ability which should never be neglected.

Let us all preserve and protect this magnificent dog The Giant Schnauzer and its heritage as a working dog.

Schutzhund

There are three schutzhund titles: Schutzhund 1 (SchH1), Schutzhund 2 (SchH2), and Schutzhund 3 (SchH3). SchH1 is the first title and SchH3 is the most advanced. Additionally, before a dog can compete for a SchH1, he must pass a temperament test called a B or BH (*Begleithundprüfung*, which translates as "traffic-sure companion dog test"). The B tests basic obedience and sureness around strange people, strange dogs, traffic, and loud noises. A dog that exhibits excessive fear, distractibility, or aggression cannot pass the B and so cannot go on to Schutzhund.

The Schutzhund test has changed over the years. Modern Schutzhund consists of three phases: tracking, obedience, and protection. A dog must pass all three phases in one trial to be awarded a Schutzhund title. Each phase is judged on a 100-point scale. The minimum passing score is 70 for the tracking and obedience phases and 80 for the protection phase. At any time the judge may dismiss a dog for showing poor temperament, including fear or aggression.

In response to political forces in Germany, in 2004 the Verein für Deutsche Schäferhunde (SV) and the Deutscher Hundesportverein (DHV) made substantial changes to Schutzhund. The DHV adopted the Fédération Cynologique Internationale (FCI) rules that govern IPO titles, so that at least on paper the SV and DHV gave up control of the sport to the FCI. The DHV changed the name of the titles from "SchH" (Schutzhund) to "VPG" (*Vielseitigkeitsprüfung für Gebrauchshunde* which roughly translates *Versatility examination for working dogs*). The SV has retained the "SchH" title names, but otherwise conforms to the DHV/FCI rules.

Tracking

The tracking phase tests not only the dogs scenting ability, but also its mental soundness and physical endurance. In the tracking phase, a track layer walks across a field, dropping several small articles along the way. After a period of time, the dog is directed to follow the track while being followed by the handler on a 33 foot leash. When the dog finds each article he indicates it, usually by lying down with the article between his front paws. The dog is scored on how intently and carefully he follows the track and indicates the articles. The length, complexity, number of articles, and age of the track varies for each title.

Obedience

The obedience phase is done in a large field, with the dogs working in pairs. One dog is placed in a down position on the side of the field and his handler leaves him while the other dog works in the field. Then the dogs switch places. In the field, there are several heeling exercises, including heeling through a group of people. There are two or three gunshots during the heeling to test the dog's reaction to loud noises.

There are one or two recalls, three retrieves (flat, jump and A-frame), and a send out where the dog is directed to run away from the handler straight and fast and then lie down on command. Obedience is judged on the dog's accuracy and attitude. The dog must show enthusiasm. A dog that is uninterested or cowering scores poorly.

Protection

In the protection phase, the judge has an assistant, called the "decoy", who helps him test the dog's courage to protect himself and his handler and his ability to be controlled while doing so. The decoy wears a heavily padded sleeve on one arm. There are several blinds, placed where the decoy can hide, on the field. The dog is directed to search the blinds for the decoy. When he finds the decoy, he indicates this by barking. The dog must guard the decoy to prevent him from moving until recalled by his handler. There follows a series of

exercises similar to police work where the handler searches the decoy and transports him to the judge. At specified points, the decoy either attacks the dog or the handler or attempts to escape. The dog must stop the attack or the escape by biting the padded sleeve. When the attack or escape stops, the dog is commanded to "out," or release the sleeve. The dog must out or he is dismissed. At all times the dog must show the courage to engage the decoy and the temperament to obey his handler while in this high state of drive. Again, the dog must show enthusiasm. A dog that shows fear, lack of control, or inappropriate aggression is dismissed.

Giant Schnauzer Registrations 1971 - 2009

Data courtesy of the Kennel Club

UK Giant Schnauzer Champions

From the very first to the very latest UK champions
in chronological order

CH SCHOLTEN STAINLESS STEEL
The First UK Champion
DOB: 27/04/1973 ♀ Pepper & Salt
Breeder: Mrs A Gwinnell
Owner: Mrs A Gwinnell
Sire: Dondeau Strathconaglen Bit
Dam: Scholten Sable Queen

Gained Title: 21/05/1977

CH ISARA DIABLO
The First UK Male Champion
DOB: 04/03/1976 ♂ Black
Breeder: Mrs F Roberts
Owner: Mrs C Derwent
Sire: Dondeau Strathconaglen Bit
Dam: Odivane Modern Milly

Gained Title: 19/05/1978

CH & NOR CH GULDMANDSBUKTENS WENCHE OF NENEVALE (IMP NORWAY)
The First UK Import Champion
DOB: 27/06/1973 ♀ Black
Breeder: S Egnaes
Owner: Mrs J C Harrison-Smith
Sire: INT CH Riesengardens Xo
Dam: NOR CH Tina

Gained Title: 01/07/1978

CH NIXADOR BLACK FANTASY OF NENEVALE

DOB: 28/03/1974 ♀ Black
Breeder: Mrs T Jefferys
Owner: Mrs J C Harrison-Smith
Sire: Scholten Ace Of Spades
Dam: Lara Of Nixador

Gained Title: 28/08/1978

CH ISARA FLORA OF PARISGARDEN

DOB: 13/06/1977 ♀ Black
Breeder: Mrs F Roberts
Owner: Mrs C Derwent
Sire: Ajax Of Isara (Imp Czechoslovakia)
Dam: Odivane Modern Milly

CH AMBASSADOR OF CATALANTA

DOB: 09/04/1977 ♂ Black
Breeder: Mrs S Hammarstrom
Owner: Mr & Mrs S Saville
Sire: AM CH Skansen's Toma
Dam: Skansen's Pretty Liv CD

CH NENEVALE BEDAZZLE

DOB: 02/09/1978 ♀ Black
Breeder: Mrs J C Harrison-Smith
Owner: Mr & Mrs J E Ward
Sire: CH Ambasador Of Catalanta
Dam: CH & NOR CH Guldmandsbuktens Wenche Of Nenevale (Imp Norway)

Gained Title: 01/12/1979

CH MYRKARBY TOMTEN-HUGO OF NENEVALE (IMP NORWAY)
DOB: 15/11/1978 ♂ Black
Breeder: V Erikson
Owner: Mrs J C Harrison-Smith
Sire: NOR CH Alko
Dam: Hedi v Buck

CH NENEVALE BUMPER BUNDLE
DOB: 02/09/1978 ♂ Black
Breeder: Mrs J C Harrison-Smith
Owner: Mrs P Redfern-Smith
Sire: CH Ambasador Of Catalanta
Dam: CH & NOR CH Guldmansbuktens Wenche Of Nenevale (Imp Norway)

CH SANDRIDGE SCHWARZE ANNI
DOB: 29/04/1980 ♀ Black
Breeder: Mr & Mrs J R Steele
Owner: Mr & Mrs J R Steele
Sire: CH Ambasador Of Catalanta
Dam: Odivane Calico Of Sandridge

CH NENEVALE DAWNBREAKER OF SIONBURGH
DOB: 12/02/1980 ♀ Black
Breeder: Mrs J C Harrison-Smith
Owner: R Patton
Sire: CH Nenevale Bumper Bundle
Dam: Nenevale Asta

CH NENEVALE ESCAPADE
DOB: 02/05/1980 ♂ Black
Breeder: Mrs J C Harrison-Smith
Owner: Mr & Mrs J Ward
Sire: CH Myrkarby Tomten-Hugo Of Nenevale (Imp Norway)
Dam: CH & NOR CH Guldmandsbuktens Wenche Of Nenevale (Imp Norway)

CH NENEVALE GOSSIP
DOB: 23/02/1981 ♀ Black
Breeder: Mrs J C Harrison-Smith
Owner: Mrs J C Harrison-Smith
Sire: CH Myrkarby Tomten-Hugo Of Nenevale (Imp Norway)
Dam: Nenevale Asta

CH NENEVALE ROXELLA RIO
DOB: 24/04/1981 ♀ Black
Breeder: Mr & Mrs J Ward
Owner: Mr & Mrs J Krall
Sire: CH Nenevale Escapade
Dam: CH Nenevale Bedazzle

Gained Title: 04/03/1984
Samoyed Association

CH ROXELLA RICOCHET OF DICARL
DOB: 28/04/1981 ♂ Black
Breeder: Mr & Mrs J Ward
Owner: Mrs D Johnson
Sire: CH Nenevale Escapade
Dam: CH Nenevale Bedazzle

CH CLEOPATRA FROM ODIVANE
DOB: 29/04/1980 ♀ Black
Breeder: Mr & Mrs J R Steele
Owner: Mrs P M Moore
Sire: CH Ambasador Of Catalanta
Dam: Odivane Calico Of Sandridge

CH NIXADOR BLACK SARACEN
DOB: 18/10/1979 ♂ Black
Breeder: Mrs T Jeffreys
Owner: Mrs T Jeffreys
Sire: CH Nenevale Bumper Bundle
Dam: Nixador Black Melody

CH PARISGARDEN DELILAH
DOB: 17/09/1980 ♀ Black
Breeder: C Derwent & Miss M Lester
Owner: C Derwent & Miss M Lester
Sire: CH Nenevale Bumper Bundle
Dam: Parisgarden Demonia

CH NENEVALE JUPITER OF LAURILL
DOB: 31/03/1982 ♂ Black
Breeder: Mrs J C Harrison-Smith
Owner: Mrs L Green
Sire: CH Ambasador Of Catalanta
Dam: Nenevale Eclipse

CH NENEVALE JUBILATION
DOB: 31/03/1982 ♀ Black
Breeder: Mrs J C Harrison-Smith
Owner: S Wareing
Sire: CH Ambasador Of Catalanta
Dam: Nenevale Eclipse

CH JANNEM TARQUIN
DOB: 27/05/1983 ♂ Black
Breeder: Mrs J Hakki
Owner: T Radford
Sire: CH Nenevale Bumper Bundle
Dam: Kilcroft Black Diamonds

Gained Title: 26/08/1985
Leicester City Canine Society

CH NENEVALE MISS MONEYPENNY
DOB: 04/07/1983 ♀ Black
Breeder: Mrs J C Harrison-Smith
Owner: Mrs D Brixey
Sire: CH Nenevale Jupiter Of Laurill
Dam: Nenevale Asta

Gained Title: 19/10/1985
Giant Schnauzer Club

CH JANNEM TESHEKKUR
DOB: 27/05/1983 ♀ Black
Breeder: Mrs J Hakki
Owner: Mrs J Hakki
Sire: CH Nenevale Bumper Bundle
Dam: Kilcroft Black Diamonds

Gained Title: 07/02/1986 Crufts

CH ROSAPIK OTHELLO OF KANIX (IMP FINLAND)
DOB: 07/04/1984 ♂ Black
Breeder: Mr & Mrs R Hagstrom
Owner: Mrs K Wilberg
Sire: Dojan v Breitenstein
Dam: Rosapik Romy

Gained Title: 19/07/1986
NW&P Breeds Dog Society

CH JAFRAK RIO GRANDE
DOB: 03/06/1984 ♀ Black
Breeder: Mr & Mrs J Krall
Owner: Mr & Mrs J Krall
Sire: CH Nenevale Jupiter Of Laurill
Dam: CH Nenevale Roxella Rio

Gained Title: 29/08/1986
City Of Birmingham Canine Association

CH SANDRIDGE GUILIETTA AT KIPFENBERG
DOB: 12/06/1985 ♀ Black
Breeder: Mr & Mrs J R Steele
Owner: Mr & Mrs R Kiesslinger
Sire: CH Rosapik Othello Of Kanix (Imp Finland)
Dam: Skansens Gretel v Guint At Sandridge (Imp USA)

Gained Title: 03/07/1987
Windsor Dog Show Society

CH NENEVALE YVETTE
DOB: 07/06/1985 ♀ Black
Breeder: Mrs J C Harrison-Smith
Owner: Mrs J C Harrison-Smith
Sire: CH Rospik Othello Of Kanix (Imp Finland)
Dam: Nenevale Kaleidoscope

Gained Title: 31/08/1987
Leicester City Canine Society

CH DICARL BLACK ADDER AT HAWNELANDS
DOB: 20/08/1985 ♂ Black
Breeder: Mrs D M Johnson
Owner: Mrs L Reaney
Sire: CH Rosapik Othello Of Kanix (Imp Finland)
Dam: Dicarl Black Satin

Gained Title: 31/08/1987 Leicester City Canine Society

CH NENEVALE YESTERDAY MAN
DOB: 07/06/1985 ♂ Black
Breeder: Mrs J C Harrison-Smith
Owner: Mrs J C Harrison-Smith
Sire: CH Rosapik Othello Of Kanix (Imp Finland)
Dam: Nenevale Kaleidoscope

Gained Title: 04/09/1987
City Of Birmingham Canine Association

CH RILLATON MISTY SHADOW
The First Pepper/Salt Male Champion
DOB: 21/04/1985 ♂ Pepper & Salt
Breeder: Mrs D Hounslow
Owner: Mrs & Mrs P Key
Sire: INT CH Adonis Van De Havenstad (Imp Belgium)
Dam: Kiznic Kalypso

Gained Title: 11/02/1988 Crufts

CH NENEVALE YVONNE
DOB: 07/06/1985 ♀ Black
Breeder: Mrs J C Harrison-Smith
Owner: Mrs J C Harrison-Smith
Sire: CH Rosapik Othello Of Kanix (Imp Finland)
Dam: Nenevale Kaleidoscope

Gained Title: 01/07/1988
Windsor Dog Show Society

CH DICARL BLACK PANTHER
DOB: 25/08/1985 ♂ Black
Breeder: Mrs D M Johnson
Owner: Mr R G Snowden
Sire: CH Rosapik Othello Of Kanix (Imp Finland)
Dam: Dicarl Black Satin

Gained Title: 23/07/1988
Leeds City & District Canine Association

CH JANNEM SADIK
DOB: 13/06/1985 ♂ Black
Breeder: Mrs J Hakki
Owner: Mr A Cuthberson
Sire: CH Rosapik Othello Of Kanix (Imp Finland)
Dam: Jannem Toska

Gained Title: 19/08/1988
Welsh Kennel Club

CH SANDRIDGE KIRRY
DOB: 17/06/1986 ♀ Black
Breeder: Mr & Mrs J R Steele
Owner: Mr & Mrs J R Steele
Sire: CH Rosapik Othello Of Kanix (Imp Finland)
Dam: Skansens Gretel v Quint At Sandridge (Imp USA)

Gained Title: 29/08/1988
Leicester City Canine Society

CH SANDRIDGE OLYMPIC GOLD
DOB: 28/07/1987 ♂ Black
Breeder: Mr & Mrs J R Steele
Owner: Mr & Mrs J R Steele
Sire: Shinlah vd Noorderenk at Nixador (Imp Holland)
Dam: Sandridge Georgia

Gained Title: 15/07/1989
NW&P Breeds Dog Society

CH NENEVALE JAMES BOND OF SCHABAAL

DOB: 27/11/1987 ♂ Black
Breeder: Mrs J C Harrison-Smith
Owner: Mrs D Brixey
Sire: CH Nenevale Yesterday Man
Dam: Jetstream Black Chiffon At Nenevale

Gained Title: 22/07/1989
Leeds City & District Canine Association

CH JAFRAK BIRD IN THE HAND

DOB: 24/04/1987 ♀ Black
Breeder: Mr & Mrs J Krall
Owner: Mr & Mrs Krall
Sire: Skansens Solstrand Handsome (Imp USA)
Dam: CH Nenevale Roxella Rio

Gained Title: 21/10/1989
Giant Schnauzer Club

CH PARISGARDEN WILLIAM

DOB: 17/12/1985 ♂ Black
Breeder: Major C S Derwent F.R.I.B.A
Owner: Mr G Flyckt-Pederson
Sire: CH Rosapik Othello Of Kanix (Imp Finland)
Dam: CH Parisgarden Delilah

Gained Title: 21/10/1989 Giant Schnauzer Club

CH NENEVALE CARMEN OF LAURILL

DOB: 20/06/1986 ♀ Black
Breeder: Mrs J C Harrison-Smith
Owner: Mrs L Green
Sire: CH Nenevale Yesterday Man
Dam: Tanya v Gunterstal At Nenevale
(Imp Switzerland)

Gained Title: 03/05/1990
Birmingham Dog Show Society Ltd

CH SANDRIDGE OH SO SHARP
DOB: 28/07/1987 ♀ Black
Breeder: Mr & Mrs J R Steele
Owner: Mr & Mrs K M Chamberlain
Sire: Shinlah vd Noorderenk at Nixador
(Imp Holland)
Dam: Sandridge Georgia

Gained Title: 22/06/1990
Blackpool & District Canine Society

CH NENEVALE ZIRA OF GILCORU
DOB: 09/10/1985 ♀ Black
Breeder: Mrs J C Harrison-Smith
Owner: Mr & Mrs G Rual
Sire: CH Nenevale Jupiter Of Laurill
Dam: Nenevale Horizon

Gained Title: 20/10/1990 Giant Schnauzer Club

CH SALTBAY KNOCK EM FOR SIX
DOB: 02/08/1988 ♀ Black
Breeder: Mrs D M Salt
Owner: Mrs D M Salt
Sire: CH Sandridge Olympic Gold
Dam: Jafrak Ed Held High of Saltby

Gained Title: 11/11/1990 Northern Schnauzer Club

CH & AM CH ZANTANAS GO FOR IT V YOULENE (IMP SWEDEN)
DOB: 05/05/1986 ♂ Black
Breeder: Mr & Mrs Uddenholm
Owner: Mr & Mrs J Krall
Sire: Zantanas Darth Wedar Of Ifni
Dam: Zantanas Youlene

Gained Title: 09/01/1991
Crufts

CH SANDRIDGE VIKTORIA AT KANIX
DOB: 09/02/1989 ♀ Black
Breeder: Mr & Mrs J R Steele
Owner: Mrs K S Wilberg
Sire: Erik De Barba Negra At Kanix (Imp Spain)
Dam: CH Sandridge Kirry

Gained Title: 23/03/1991 Schnauzer Club Of Great Britain

CH XEROS V BUCK OF NENEVALE (IMP GERMANY)
DOB: 12/10/1989 ♂ Black
Breeder: Mr R Dietsche-Lötscher
Owner: Mrs J C Harrison-Smith
Sire: DUTCH CH Elzar V Bergherbos
Dam: GERM CH Nenevale Arina

Gained Title: 16/05/1991
Scottish Kennel Club

CH BOUJAN THE ABSOLUTE LIMIT
DOB: 18/12/1988 ♂ Black
Breeder: Mr & Mrs F Boulton
Owner: Mr & Mrs F Boulton
Sire: CH Nenvale Yesterday Man
Dam: Nenevale Uta

Gained Title: 24/05/1991
Bath Canine Society

CH SANDRIDGE ANNE MARIE
DOB: 26/04/1990 ♀ Black
Breeder: Mr & Mrs J R Steele
Owner: Mrs L Steele
Sire: SP CH Vania De Pichera
Dam: CH Sandridge Kirry

Gained Title: 27/07/1991
Leeds City & District Canine Association

CH SANDRIDGE ALBERTO AT KANIX
DOB: 26/04/1990 ♂ Black
Breeder: Mr & Mrs J R Steele
Owner: Mrs L Casali
Sire: SP CH Vania De Pichera
Dam: CH Sandrige Kirry

Gained Title: 04/08/1991 Giant Schnauzer Club

CH NENEVALE VISTA
DOB: 03/09/1989 ♂ Black
Breeder: Mrs J C Harrison-Smith
Owner: Mrs S K Vaughan
Sire: CH Nenevale Yesterday Man
Dam: Nenevale Anika

Gained Title: 09/01/1992
Crufts

CH NENEVALE U KNOW AT SPRINGFLITE
DOB: 27/07/1989 ♀ Black
Breeder: Mrs J C Harrison-Smith
Owner: Messrs M Butler & K Dodd
Sire: Nenevale Narrator
Dam: Nenevale Kaleidoscope

Gained Title: 03/07/1992
Windsor Dog Show Society

CH NENEVALE CASANOVA AT LAURILL
DOB: 07/02/1991 ♂ Black
Breeder: Mrs J C Harrison-Smith
Owner: Mesdames L Y Green & J C Harrison-Smith
Sire: CH Xeros v Buck Of Nenevale (Imp Germany)
Dam: Nenevale Kaleidoscope

Gained Title: 18/07/1992
NW&P Breeds Dog Society

CH NENEVALE ABRACADABRA FOR BOUJAN

DOB: 05/08/1990 ♀ Black
Breeder: Mrs J C Harrison-Smith
Owner: Mr & Mrs F Boulton
Sire: Password v Bergherbos To Nenevale (Imp Holland)
Dam: Nenevale Pussy Galore

Gained Title: 19/09/1992
Darlington Dog Show Society

CH ISARA QUELLA AT NIXADOR

DOB: 15/02/1991 ♀ Pepper & Salt
Breeder: Mrs F Roberts
Owner: Mrs T Jefferys
Sire: Rillaton Misty Chief At Nixador
Dam: Isara Minerva

Gained Title: 28/05/1993 Bath Canine Society

CH SANDRIDGE ANASTASIA

DOB: 26/04/1990 ♀ Black
Breeder: Mr & Mrs J R Steele
Owner: Mrs J A Stanley
Sire: SP CH Vania De Pichera
Dam: CH Sandrige Kirry

Gained Title: 05/06/1993 Southern Counties Canine Association

CH STABLEMASTERS EX LEE (IMP FINLAND)

DOB: 30/09/1990 ♂ Black
Breeder: Ms F Faberge
Owner: Mrs D Hounslow
Sire: Quintus V Bergherbos
Dam: Riesenhoff Ziggy Twiggy

Gained Title: 25/06/1993
Blackpool & District Canine Society

CH NENEVALE VOGUE
DOB: 03/09/1989 ♀ Black
Breeder: Mrs J C Harrison-Smith
Owner: Mr & Mrs W Rylance
Sire: CH Nenevale Yesterday Man
Dam: Nenevale Anika

Gained Title: 20/08/1993
Welsh Kennel Club

CH NENEVALE FLOWER POWER OF SPRINGFLITE
DOB: 15/09/1991 ♀ Black
Breeder: Mrs J C Harrison-Smith
Owner: Messrs M Butler & K Dodd
Sire: CH Xeros v Buck of Nenevale (Imp Germany)
Dam: Nenevale Quedo

Gained Title: 20/08/1993
Schnauzer Club Of Great Britain

CH WILDENRATH GOLDFINGER
DOB: 09/11/1988 ♂ Black
Breeder: Mr & Mrs L Willoughby
Owner: Mr L Willoughby
Sire: Dicarl Black Mamba
Dam: Nenevale Dolley Daydream

Gained Title: 19/08/1994
Welsh Kennel Club

CH SANDRIDGE ALEXANDRA
DOB: 26/04/1990 ♀ Black
Breeder: Mr & Mrs J R Steele
Owner: Mr B Berger
Sire: SP CH Vania De Pichera
Dam: CH Sandrige Kirry

Gained Title: 19/08/1994 Welsh Kennel Club

CH JAFRAK KEEP COOL

DOB: 11/10/1993 ♂ Black
Breeder: Mr & Mrs J Krall
Owner: Mr & Mrs Krall
Sire: Skansens Quality At Zantana (Imp USA)
Dam: Jafrak For Keeps

Gained Title: 25/03/1995
Schnauzer Club Of Great Britain

CH JAFRAK KEEP TALKING

DOB: 11/10/1993 ♀ Black
Breeder: Mr & Mrs J Krall
Owner: Mr & Mrs S Wareing
Sire: Skansens Quality At Zantana (Imp USA)
Dam: Jafrak For Keeps

Gained Title: 12/05/1995
Birmingham Dog Show Society Ltd

CH NENEVALE FRONT RUNNER

DOB: 15/09/1991 ♂ Black
Breeder: Mrs J C Harrison-Smith
Owner: Mr P Clayton & Miss J Hodges
Sire: CH Xeros V Buck Of Nenevale (Imp Germany)
Dam: Nenevale Quedo

Gained Title: 18/08/1995 Welsh Kennel Club

CH FOXWOOD DOUBLE EDGED

DOB: 07/02/1993 ♂ Black
Breeder: Mr & Mrs W Rylance
Owner: Mr & Mrs W Rylance
Sire: CH Xeros V Buck Of Nenevale (Imp Germany)
Dam: CH Nenevale Vogue

Gained Title: 22/10/1995
Giant Schnauzer Club

CH JAFRAK SEE IF I CARE
DOB: 22/05/1993 ♂ Black
Breeder: Mr & Mrs J Krall
Owner: Mrs J Tucker
Sire: Jafrak Handle With Care
Dam: Jafrak Go Ask Alice

Gained Title: 01/06/1996
Southern Counties Canine Association

CH FOXWOOD DOUBLE ENTENDRE AT ZANCLUS
DOB: 07/02/1993 ♀ Black
Breeder: Mr & Mrs W Rylance
Owner: Mr & Mrs R Cook
Sire: CH Xeros V Buck Of Nenevale (Imp Germany)
Dam: CH Nenevale Vogue

Gained Title: 21/06/1996 Blackpool & District Canine Society

CH JAFRAK CALIFORNIA DREAMIN
DOB: 26/04/1995 ♀ Black
Breeder: Mr & Mrs J Krall
Owner: Mr & Mrs Krall
Sire: CH Jafrak Keep Cool
Dam: Skansens Quality At Jafrak (Imp USA)

Gained Title: 20/10/1996
Giant Schnauzer Club

CH NENEVALE LANDMAKER
DOB: 01/09/1993 ♂ Black
Breeder: Mrs J C Harrison-Smith
Owner: Mr K Rofe-Moss
Sire: CH Nenevale Casanova At Laurill
Dam: Xyla V Buck Of Nenevale (Imp Germany)

Gained Title: 06/06/1997
Southern Counties Canine Association

CH NENEVALE OTTO MEIN-HERR

DOB: 26/08/1994 ♂ Black
Breeder: Mrs J C Harrison-Smith
Owner: Mrs M Twycross
Sire: CH Nenevale Vista
Dam: Nenevale Isadora

Gained Title: 04/07/1997 Windsor Dog Show Society

CH FOXWOOD TOP SPEED

DOB: 09/01/1995 ♂ Black
Breeder: Mr & Mrs W Rylance
Owner: Mr & Mrs W Rylance
Sire: CH Foxwood Double Edged
Dam: Nenevale Justeenia

Gained Title: 15/08/1997
Welsh Kennel Club

CH PENBRO DESTINIES DAUGHTER

DOB: 26/04/1994 ♀ Black
Breeder: Ms L Grimmett
Owner: Ms L Grimmett
Sire: CH Stablemasters Ex Lee (Imp Finland)
Dam: Rillaton Dutch Gal of Penbro

Gained Title: 19/10/1997
Giant Schnauzer Club

CH FOXWOOD INCOGNITO

DOB: 28/08/1996 ♂ Black
Breeder: Mr & Mrs W Rylance
Owner: Mr & Mrs Maggs
Sire: Donjuan De Pichera At Foxwood (Imp Spain)
Dam: Foxwood Cosmopolitan

Gained Title: 07/05/1998
Birmingham Dog Show Society Ltd

CH NENEVALE RAZZLE-DAZZLE RIESENHEIM
DOB: 23/09/1995 ♀ Black
Breeder: Mrs J C Harrison-Smith
Owner: Mr K Rofe-Moss
Sire: Foxwood Pacco Rabane
Dam: Nenevale Isadora

Gained Title: 07/05/1998
Birmingham Dog Show Society Ltd

CH JANNEM MUMTEREM
DOB: 09/10/1993 ♂ Black
Breeder: Mrs J A Hakki
Owner: Mrs J Habbin
Sire: Skansens Quality At Zantana (Imp USA)
Dam: Jannem Tanya

Gained Title: 22/05/1998
Bath Canine Society

CH NENEVALE QUIP MODEST
DOB: 11/09/1995 ♂ Black
Breeder: Mrs J C Harrison-Smith
Owner: Mr & Mrs Crocket
Sire: Nenevale Artois
Dam: Foxwood Double Trouble At Nenevale

Gained Title: 08/11/1998 Northern Schnauzer Club

CH JAFRAK ZUCCHINI
DOB: 05/11/1996 ♂ Black
Breeder: Mr & Mrs J Krall
Owner: Mr K Cullen & Mrs A Heard
Sire: Skansen's Tortellini at Jafrak (Imp USA)
Dam: Skansens Quality at Jafrak (Imp USA)

Gained Title: 11/12/1998
Ladies Kennel Association

CH JAFRAK POP THE QUESTION
DOB: 16/06/1996 ♀ Black
Breeder: Mr & Mrs J Krall
Owner: Mr & Mrs J Krall
Sire: Skansens Tortellini At Jafrak
Dam: Jafrak Keep Laughing

Gained Title: 28/05/1999
Bath Canine Society

CH SPRINGFLITE OUT OF THE BLUE
DOB: 16/06/1996 ♀ Black
Breeder: Mr K Dodd & Mr M Butler
Owner: Mr K Dodd & Mr M Butler
Sire: Donjuan De Pichera At Foxwood (Imp Spain)
Dam: CH Nenevale Flower Power of Springflite

Gained Title: 17/07/1999
NW&P Breeds Dog Society

CH INDIGO CHIEF FOXWOOD
DOB: 19/09/1997 ♂ Black
Breeder: Mr & Mrs Fewings
Owner: Ms N Rylance & Mrs L Welch
Sire: Donjuan De Pichera At Foxwood (Imp Spain)
Dam: Nenevale Loretta

Gained Title: 24/07/1999
Leeds City & District Canine Association

CH JAFRAK DOLCELATA
DOB: 05/11/1996 ♀ Black
Breeder: Mr & Mrs J Krall
Owner: Mr & Mrs K Cullen
Sire: Skansens Tortellini At Jafrak (Imp USA)
Dam: Skansens Quality At Jafrak (Imp USA)

Gained Title: 18/09/1999
Darlington Dog Show Society

CH JAFRAK PORCINI

DOB: 05/11/1996 ♀ Black
Breeder: Mr & Mrs J Krall
Owner: Mrs M Faulkner
Sire: Skansen's Tortellini at Jafrak (Imp USA)
Dam: Skansens Quality at Jafrak (Imp USA)

Gained Title: 10/12/1999
Ladies Kennel Association

CH STABLEMASTER'S SEVENTH HEAVEN OF LEEBAY (IMP FINLAND)

DOB: 21/11/1995 ♀ Black
Breeder: Ms F Faberge
Owner: Mrs B Cocks
Sire: Friper De Pichera
Dam: Stablemaster's Electric Lady

Gained Title: 20/04/2000
Birmingham Dog Show Society Ltd

CH ZAMORANOS PICASSO

DOB: 13/06/1998 ♂ Black
Breeder: Mr A & Mrs J Alvarez
Owner: Mr A Alvarez-Campos & Mrs J Alvarez-Kefford
Sire: Donjuan De Pichera At Foxwood (Imp Spain)
Dam: Dona Truchas Juniorde Los Chapulitos

Gained Title: 15/07/2000
NW&P Breeds Dog Society

CH JAFRAK DREAM ON

DOB: 01/10/1998 ♂ Black
Breeder: Mr & Mrs J Krall
Owner: Ms T Crouch & Mr D Quigg
Sire: CH Jafrak Zucchini
Dam: CH Jafrak California Dreamin

Gained Title: 01/06/2001
Southern Counties Canine Association

CH JAFRAK DREAM COME TRUE
DOB: 01/10/1998 ♀ Black
Breeder: Mr & Mrs J Krall
Owner: Mr K Cullen & Mrs A Heard
Sire: CH Jafrak Zucchini
Dam: CH Jafrak California Dreamin

Gained Title: 01/06/2001
Southern Counties Canine Association

CH BOUJAN JUAN DA BRA
DOB: 07/03/1998 ♀ Black
Breeder: Mr F Boulton
Owner: Mr P Bagshaw & Mr F Boulton
Sire: Donjuan De Pichera At Foxwood (Imp Spain)
Dam: CH Nenevale Abracadabra for Boujan

Gained Title: 22/06/2001 Blackpool & District Canine Society

CH INGELLA FANCY DANCING OF NENEVALE
DOB: 23/03/1999 ♀ Black
Breeder: Ms I Young
Owner: Mrs J C Harrison-Smith
Sire: Hassanhills John Player Special (Imp Sweden)
Dam: Riesenheims Land Lady

Gained Title: 29/06/2001 Windsor Dog Show Society

CH RIESENHEIM CEBREROS
DOB: 10/06/1997 ♂ Black
Breeder: Mr K Rofe-Moss
Owner: Mr K Rofe-Moss
Sire: Donjuan De Pichera At Foxwood (Imp Spain)
Dam: Ferncliffe Violetta Of Nenevale

Gained Title: 17/08/2001
Welsh Kennel Club

CH JAFRAK BRUSHSTROKES
DOB: 24/04/2000 ♀ Black
Breeder: Mr & Mrs J Krall
Owner: Mr K Cullen & Mrs R Thomas
Sire: CH Zamoranos Picasso
Dam: CH Jafrak California Dreamin

Gained Title: 11/11/2001
Northern Schnauzer Club

CH FOXWOOD BUSINESS AS USUAL
DOB: 28/11/1997 ♀ Black
Breeder: Mr & Mrs W & N Rylance
Owner: Mr & Mrs K & L Hughes
Sire: Donjuan De Pichera At Foxwood
(Imp Spain)
Dam: Foxwood Cosmopolitan

Gained Title: 24/05/2002
Bath Canine Society

CH JAFRAK ANNIE GET YOUR GUN
DOB: 03/11/1999 ♀ Black
Breeder: Mr & Mrs J Krall
Owner: Mr & Mrs K Roberts
Sire: Skansens Western Cowboy At Jafrak
(Imp USA)
Dam: Ch Jafrak Pop The Question

Gained Title: 20/07/2002
NW&P Breeds Dog Society

CH JAFRAK PHILIPPE OLIVIER
Crufts Best in Show 2008
DOB: 03/04/2001 ♂ Black
Breeder: Mr & Mrs J Krall
Owner: Mr & Mrs K Cullen
Sire: Multi CH Luther King Du Bujol
Dam: CH Jafrak Dolcelata

Gained Title: 27/07/2002
Leeds City & District Canine Association

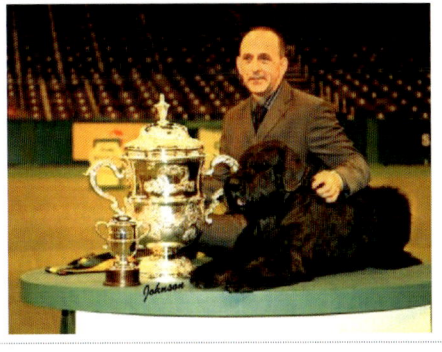

CH FERNCLIFFE'S BETE NOIRE
DOB: 20/10/1999 ♀ Black
Breeder: Mrs K A Carroll
Owner: Mrs K A Carroll
Sire: Zamoranos Dali
Dam: Ferncliffe Laquenta

Gained Title: 16/08/2002
Welsh Kennel Club

CH JAFRAK WHEEL OF FORTUNE
DOB: 13/11/2000 ♀ Black
Breeder: Mr & Mrs J Krall
Owner: Mr M G & Mrs G M Wise
Sire: Ch Jafrak Zucchini
Dam: Ch Jafrak Pop the Question

Gained Title: 12/09/2003
Darlington Dog Show Society

CH BOWENHURST SILVER BOSS
DOB: 11/11/2001 ♂ Pepper & Salt
Breeder: Mrs P Wollen
Owner: Mrs P Wollen
Sire: Rillaton Misty Mountain Lad
Dam: Bellgard Ivory Teardrops At Bowenhurst

Gained Title: 25/06/2004
Blackpool & District Canine Society

CH FOXWOOD NO REGRETS
DOB: 01/10/2000 ♀ Black
Breeder: Mr & Mrs W & N Rylance
Owner: Mr & Mrs K & L Hughes
Sire: Foreman de Lordship's Del Reisenheim (Imp Spain)
Dam: CH Foxwood Business as Usual

Gained Title: 14/11/2004
Northern Schnauzer Club

CH & IR CH RIESENHEIM MONTOYA
DOB: 04/01/2003 ♂ Black
Breeder: Mr K Rofe-Moss
Owner: Mr & Mrs N Wengler
Sire: CH Riesenheim Cebreros
Dam: Riesenheim Splashdown

Gained Title: 03/06/2005
Southern Counties Canine Association

CH HABARNY YANKEE GIGGLES
DOB: 25/03/2002 ♀ Black
Breeder: Mrs J Habbin
Owner: Ms L Bailey & Mr G Grant
Sire: Skansens Yankee Clipper At Jafrak (Imp USA)
Dam: Jafrak Joking Apart With Habarny

Gained Title: 16/07/2005
NW&P Breeds Dog Society

CH JAFRAK PHILADELPHIA
DOB: 04/12/2002 ♀ Black
Breeder: Mr & Mrs J Krall
Owner: Mr K N C & Mrs K Roberts
Sire: CH Jafrak Philippe Olivier
Dam: Jafrak Amanda Lear

Gained Title: 23/07/2005
Leeds City & District Canine Association

CH RIESENHEIM SUITED N'BOOTED FOR DALEIDEN
DOB: 21/07/2003 ♂ Black
Breeder: Mr K Rofe-Moss
Owner: Mr K Moss & Mrs M Heinz
Sire: CH Jafrak Philippe Olivier
Dam: Riesenheim Rikki Lake

Gained Title: 13/11/2005
Northern Schnauzer Club

CH RIESENHEIM VERSACE
DOB: 21/07/2003 ♀ Black
Breeder: Mr K Rofe-Moss
Owner: Mr D Grubb
Sire: CH Jafrak Philippe Olivier
Dam: Riesenheim Rikki Lake

Gained Title: 09/12/2005
Ladies Kennel Association

CH JAFRAK PHILHARMONICA
DOB: 04/12/2002 ♀ Black
Breeder: Mr & Mrs J Krall
Owner: Mr B Loving
Sire: CH Jafrak Philippe Olivier
Dam: Jafrak Amanda Lear

Gained Title: 19/01/2006
Manchester Dog Show Society

CH FOXWOOD XTRAVAGANZA
DOB: 10/11/2004 ♀ Black
Breeder: Ms N Rylance & Mr & Mrs Moore
Owner: Ms N Rylance
Sire: Riesenheim Galliano
Dam: Foxwood Strictly Business

Gained Title: 19/05/2006
Scottish Kennel Club

CH NENEVALE BELLISSIMA OF COLDNOSE
DOB: 01/08/2004 ♀ Black
Breeder: Mrs J C Harrison-Smith
Owner: Mrs J Lunn
Sire: Ferncliffe Ivan Ivanovich
Dam: CH Ingella Fancy Dancing of Nenevale

Gained Title: 23/06/2006 Blackpool & District Canine Society

CH INKA HOOTS FROM FOXWOOD
DOB: 15/11/2004 ♀ Black
Breeder: Mr & Mrs Hughes
Owner: Mrs L J Parker
Sire: CH Riesenheim Cebreros
Dam: CH Foxwood Business As Usual

Gained Title: 22/10/2006
Giant Schnauzer Club

CH RIESENHEIM CAPT FANTASTIC
DOB: 26/04/2005 ♂ Black
Breeder: Mr K Rofe-Moss
Owner: Mr K Moss & Mrs M Heinz
Sire: Top-Style Mustang At Leebay (Imp Finland)
Dam: Riesenheim Fanny Adams

Gained Title: 18/01/2007
Manchester Dog Show Society

CH JAFRAK NIPPED IN THE BUD
DOB: 21/08/2005 ♀ Black
Breeder: Mr & Mrs J Krall
Owner: Mr J Krall & Mrs S Alwyn
Sire: Skansens Ceasar
Dam: Jafrak Overnight

Gained Title: 18/05/2007
Scottish Kennel Club

CH KHINJAN CINNABAR
DOB: 06/07/2005 ♀ Black
Breeder: Mrs P A Hattrell-Tredgett
Owner: Mrs S Hattrell
Sire: Grovelea Adventurer
Dam: Ingella Coco Chanel At Khinjan

Gained Title: 22/06/2007
Blackpool & District Canine Society

CH PRIMAVISTA SOFIA LOREN
DOB: 12/02/2006 ♀ Black
Breeder: Mr M Whitney & Mr A Di Martino
Owner: Mr M Whitney & Mr A Di Martino
Sire: Craggyknowe Cheeky Chico At Primavista
Dam: Bellgard Marie Antoinette At Primavista

Gained Title: 05/07/2007
South Wales Kennel Association

CH BELLGARD PALOMA PICASSO
DOB: 12/07/2003 ♀ Black
Breeder: Mr R Joy
Owner: Mr R Joy & Mr & Mrs K Cullen
Sire: CH Zamoranos Picasso
Dam: Bellgard Ebony Navannah

Gained Title: 17/01/2008
Manchester Dog Show Society

CH FOXWOOD INDESPUTABLE AT BARNSDALE
DOB: 12/11/2005 ♂ Black
Breeder: Ms N Rylance & Mr & Mrs Moore
Owner: Mr & Mrs M & J & Ms H Houchin
Sire: Riesenheim Galliano
Dam: Foxwood Indian Summer

Gained Title: 08/05/2008
Birmingham Dog Show Society Ltd

CH JAFRAK LE FANTASIE
DOB: 25/05/2006 ♀ Black
Breeder: Mr & Mrs J Krall
Owner: Mr & Mrs Krall
Sire: CH Riesenheim Capt Fantastic
Dam: CH Jafrak Philadelphia

Gained Title: 12/07/2008
NW&P Breeds Dog Society

CH GROVELEA FOXTROT
DOB: 29/03/2006 ♀ Black
Breeder: Mrs S Cox & Mr K Bowman
Owner: Mrs S Cox & Mr K Bowman
Sire: Jafrak Over Easy
Dam: Grovelea Cha Cha

Gained Title: 12/12/2008
Ladies Kennel Association

CH BELLGARD GHETTO STILETTO AT PHILOMA
DOB: 30/06/2006 ♀ Black
Breeder: Mr R Joy
Owner: Mr & Mrs K Cullen & Mr R Joy
Sire: Bellgard Masaccio
Dam: Histyles Vanity Fair At Bellgard (Imp USA)

Gained Title: 15/01/2009
Manchester Dog Show Society

CH JAFRAK CAUSING A COMMOTION
DOB: 26/03/2006 ♂ Black
Breeder: Mr & Mrs J Krall
Owner: Mr & Mrs Krall
Sire: Skansens Yankee Clipper At Jafrak (Imp USA)
Dam: Jafrak Overnight

Gained Title: 05/06/2009
Southern Counties Canine Association

CH PRIMAVISTA RUMBA CARUMBA
DOB: 12/02/2006 ♂ Black
Breeder: Mr M Whitney & Mr A Di Martino
Owner: Mrs H J & Mr R A Smith
Sire: Craggyknowe Cheeky Chico At Primavista
Dam: Bellgard Marie Antoinette At Primavista

Gained Title: 26/06/2009
Blackpool & District Canine Society

CH & IR CH FOXWOOD BOMBSHELL
DOB: 21/11/2006 ♀ Black
Breeder: Ms N Rylance
Owner: Mr & Mrs Wengler
Sire: Gently Born Molotov at Foxwood (Imp Russia)
Dam: CH Foxwood Xtravaganza

Gained Title: 08/10/2009
South Wales Kennel Association

CH DRAXPARK BIG SHOT
The First UK Tailed Champion
DOB: 07/09/2007 ♂ Black
Breeder: Mrs L J Parker
Owner: Mrs L J Parker
Sire: CH Riesenheim Suited N'Booted For Daleiden
Dam: CH Inka Hoots From Foxwood

Gained Title: 08/10/2009
South Wales Kennel Association

CH RIESENHEIM BITE THE BULLET
DOB: 02/02/2008 ♂ Black
Breeder: Mr K Rofe-Moss
Owner: Mr K Moss & Mrs M Heinz
Sire: CH Riesenheim Suited N'Booted for Daleiden
Dam: Riesenheim Russian Rhythm

Gained Title: 25/10/2009
Giant Schnauzer Club

CH PRIMAVISTA MAMBO ITALIANO
DOB: 12/02/2006 ♂ Black
Breeder: Mr M Whitney & Mr A Di Martino
Owner: Mr M Whitney & Mr A Di Martino
Sire: Craggyknowe Cheeky Chico At Primavista
Dam: Bellgard Marie Antoinette At Primavista

Gained Title: 27/03/2010
Schnauzer Club of Great Britain

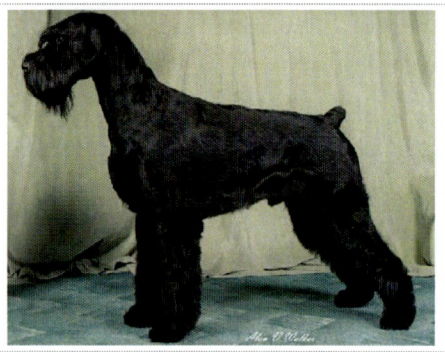

CH DRAXPARK HOT SHOT
The First UK Tailed Bitch Champion
DOB: 07/09/2007 ♀ Black
Breeder: Mrs L J Parker
Owner: Mrs L J Parker
Sire: CH Riesenheim Suited N'Booted For Daleiden
Dam: CH Inka Hoots From Foxwood

Gained Title: 17/07/2010
NW&P Breeds Dog Society

UK Giant Schnauzer Imports

From the very first to the very latest UK imports in chronological order

Information Copyright the Kennel Club

Information up to 1999 reproduced from the Giant Schnauzer Club 1999 Handbook. Information 1999-2009 reproduced with permission of the Kennel Club.

RIESENGARDENS KING OF PUSZTAMERGES
♂ Black
Country of Origin: Sweden
Breeder: E & B Ohberg
Owner: D Becker
Sire: Groll vd Reusenburg
Dam: Riesengardens Bogey

WIGSANDS ILSE
♀ Black
Country of Origin: Sweden
Breeder:
Owner: D Becker
Sire: FIN CH Bento
Dam: FIN CH Skallorns Ringa

BRUTUS VD CLEYBURCH FROM ODIVANE

DOB: 07/08/1971 ♂ Pepper & Salt
Country of Origin: Holland
Breeder: J W Merch
Owner: Mrs P M Moore
Sire: Kamp Akim vd Cleyburch
Dam: Ondra v Widderhof

ANCARA VD POPULERIEN

DOB: 27/12/1969 ♀ Black
Country of Origin: Holland
Breeder: D Harten
Owner: Mrs S Gwynne-Williams
Sire: Bill v Schneiderstein
Dam: Cyntha vd Drei Harten

KIMBO AV INGEHALL OF PENBARI

DOB: 19/01/1970 ♂ Pepper & Salt
Country of Origin: Denmark
Breeder: Mrs B Barro
Owner: Mrs C Williams
Sire: Marko vd Lonrquelle
Dam: Kinnie AV Inglehall

MALYA FANTOMAS

DOB: 28/08/1971 ♂ Black
Country of Origin: Italy
Breeder: Mrs Pozzi
Owner: Mrs A Gwinnell & Mrs R Maher
Sire: Camp Coli Della Scalla
Dam: Camp Delia Dei Diavoli Neri

BERTHE DE LA BRETCHE OF BURSTON
DOB: 12/12/1975 ♀ Black
Country of Origin: USA
Breeder: H J & E W Cordell
Owner: Mrs M Seed
Sire: Le Charbon De La Bretche
Dam: De La Bretche Eugenie

INT CH ENGHELBERTO FROM ODIVANE
DOB: 12/06/1976 ♂ Black
Country of Origin: Italy
Breeder: Dr Rossi
Owner: Mrs P M Moore
Sire: Brenno Di Torre Del Monta
Dam: Veroushka Dei Margravi

AJAX OF ISARA
DOB: 30/04/1976 ♂ Black
Country of Origin: Czechoslovakia
Breeder: Mrs Bednarova
Owner: Mrs F Roberts
Sire: INT CH Kara v Lobbachtal
Dam: Hessy v Olmeru

NOR CH GULDMANDSBUKTENS WENCHE OF NENEVALE
DOB: 27/06/1973 ♀ Black
Country of Origin: Norway
Breeder: S Egnaes
Owner: Mrs J C Harrison-Smith
Sire: INT CH Riesengardens Xo
Dam: NOR CH Tina

SKANSENS PRETTY LIV
DOB: 23/11/1974 ♀ Black
Country of Origin: USA
Breeder: Mrs S Hammarstrom
Owner: Mrs S Hammarstrom
Sire: AM CH Fancways Columbo
Dam: AM CH & CAN CH Skansens Nya Topaz

SKANSENS BLACK OPAL
DOB: 11/07/1977 ♀ Black
Country of Origin: USA
Breeder: Mrs S Hammarstrom
Owner: Mrs D Kenis
Sire: AM CH Jay-Starr's Aquarius
Dam: AM & CAN CH Skansens Nya Topaz

MYRKARBY TOMTEN-HUGO OF NENEVALE
DOB: 15/11/1978 ♂ Black
Country of Origin: Norway
Breeder: V Erikson
Owner: Mrs J C Harrison-Smith
Sire: NOR CH Alko
Dam: Hedi v Buck

VESTRIESENS BOLLE
DOB: 12/09/1978 ♂ Black
Country of Origin: Finland
Breeder: N P Hansen
Owner: R W Wiggin
Sire: Asterix Quinto
Dam: Anja

HANNAH VON ELBE
DOB: 20/08/1976 ♀ Black
Country of Origin: Canada
Breeder: A J Von Elbe
Owner: Mrs S Hutchinson
Sire: AM CH El Lobo Emo
Dam: Krisja Von Sheepstead

RICO MONTEBELLO AT NENEVALE
DOB: 09/05/1982 ♂ Black
Country of Origin: Switzerland
Breeder: Mr & Mrs A Balsieger
Owner: Mrs J C Harrison-Smith
Sire: Maik V Klybeck
Dam: Esta c Lobbachtal

DORRY VD HAVENSTAD OF BURSTON
DOB: 15/11/1979 ♀ Pepper & Salt
Country of Origin: Belgium
Breeder: C De Meulenaer
Owner: Mrs M Seed
Sire: CH Yari vd Heegh
Dam: Yolli vd Bergskens

SKANSENS SOLSTSRAND QUINCY
DOB: 13/08/1982 ♂ Black
Country of Origin: USA
Breeder: Mrs S Hammarstrom
Owner: Mrs D Kenis
Sire: AM CH & DT CH Quint v Lobbachtal
Dam: AM CH Skansens Daphne v Kobuch

SKANSENS GRETEL V QUINT AT SANDRIDGE
DOB: 18/10/1982 ♀ Black
Country of Origin: USA
Breeder: Mrs S Hammarstrom
Owner: Mr & Mrs J R Steele
Sire: AM CH & GERM CH Quint v Lobbachtal
Dam: AM CH Skansens Dockan v Kobuch

GERM CH ILLO V GUNTERSTAL AT NENEVALE
DOB: 28/09/1978 ♂ Black
Country of Origin: Germany
Breeder: Mr & Mrs R & E Hartmann
Owner: Mrs J C Harrison-Smith
Sire: GERM CH Arko v Hurblsbach
Dam: GERM CH Isabell v Aronsfeld

INT CH ADONIS VD HAVENSTAD
DOB: 12/07/1976 ♂ Pepper & Salt
Country of Origin: Belgium
Breeder: C De Meulenaer
Owner: Mrs A Gwinnell & Mrs T Jefferys
Sire: Wasko vd Ruighonk
Dam: Yolli vd Bergskens

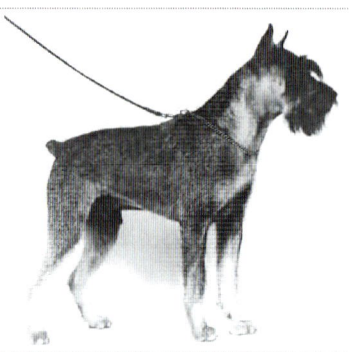

RUFUS DU BUJOL
DOB: 15/08/1980 ♂ Black
Country of Origin: France
Breeder: P Jolibois
Owner: Mr & Mrs D M Stahl
Sire: L'Nero v Krayenrain
Dam: Mussa De Nicklausbrunn

WAREHEIM LEADER OF ZOLTANIKA
DOB: 30/10/1983 ♂ Black
Country of Origin: South Africa
Breeder: Mr & Mrs J Gallant
Owner: G Green
Sire: Ilke vd Lederhecke
Dam: CH Cora Van't Wareheim

SKANSENS SOLSTRAND HANDSOME
DOB: 28/12/1983 ♂ Black
Country of Origin: USA
Breeder: Mrs S Hammarstrom
Owner: Mrs D Kenis
Sire: AM CH Skansens Der Figaro v Kobuch
Dam: AM CH Skansens Black Kajsa v Columbo

SKANSENS JAFRAK HAPPINESS
DOB: 28/12/1983 ♀ Black
Country of Origin: USA
Breeder: Mrs S Hammarstrom
Owner: Mr & Mrs Krall
Sire: AM CH Skansens Der Fiagro v Kobuch
Dam: AM CH Skansens Black Kajsa v Columbo

FLOE V BUCK OF NENEVALE
DOB: 14/04/1984 ♀ Black
Country of Origin: Germany
Breeder: R Dietsche-Lötscher
Owner: N Foster
Sire: Nenevale Icarus
Dam: Ora v Buck

INTOUCHABLE VD HAVENSTAD OF BURSTON
DOB: 20/03/1984 ♂ Pepper & Salt
Country of Origin: Belgium
Breeder: C De Meulenaer
Owner: Mrs M Seed
Sire: INT CH Faust vd Havenstad
Dam: Graaskaggs Bonni

ROSAPIK OTHELLO OF KANIX
DOB: 07/04/1984 ♂ Black
Country of Origin: Finland
Breeder: Mr & Mrs R Hagstrom
Owner: Mrs K S Wilberg
Sire: Dogan v Breitenstein
Dam: Rosapik Romy

JOSEPHIN V BUCK AT NENEVALE
DOB: 17/12/1984 ♀ Black
Country of Origin: Germany
Breeder: R Dietsche-Lötscher
Owner: Mrs J C Harrison-Smith
Sire: GERM CH Chico v Buck
Dam: Zilla v Buck

JUST V BUCK AT NENEVALE
DOB: 17/12/1984 ♂ Black
Country of Origin: Germany
Breeder: R Dietsche-Lötscher
Owner: Mrs J C Harrison-Smith
Sire: GERM CH Chico v Buck
Dam: Zilla v Buck

TANYA V GUNTERSTAL AT NENEVALE
DOB: 29/03/1983 ♀ Black
Country of Origin: Switzerland
Breeder: R Hartman
Owner: Mrs J C Harrison-Smith
Sire: GERM CH Illo v Gunterstal At Nenevale
Dam: GERM CH Uschi v Gunterstal

ASTOR V WASBEKERMOOR
DOB: 23/09/1985
Country of Origin: Germany
Breeder: Dr J Frahm
Owner: Mr M Pole
Sire: Pollux v Nygemunster
Dam: Venni v Sielbeck Uklei

SHINDAH VD NOORDERNEK AT NIXADOR
DOB: 09/05/1986 ♂
Country of Origin: Holland
Breeder: Mr J Liet
Owner: Mrs T Jefferys
Sire: DUTCH CH Ajoeri vd Reenhorst
Dam: Livette vd Noordernek

VOMBUSCHLAND MERRY
DOB: 22/12/1984
Country of Origin: South Africa
Breeder: Mr M L Ninke
Owner: Mrs S Nirch
Sire: Pit Vom Kapellenberg
Dam: Warenheim Faleska vom Buschland

EXPLOSIV'S CIRASS OF BURSTON
DOB: 22/07/1986
Country of Origin: Sweden
Breeder: Ms L Karlstrom
Owner: Mrs M Seed
Sire: Explosiv's Macsimillian
Dam: Explosiv's Postilla

ERIK DE BARBA NEGRA AT KANIX
DOB: 14/03/1986 Black
Country of Origin: Spain
Breeder: Mr J Sanchez
Owner: Mrs K Wilberg
Sire: SPAN CH Michell vd Hohen Ward
Dam: SPAN CH Pia Gunterstal

KNUT VON DER EDERTALSPERRE OF BURSTON
DOB: 25/09/1986 Pepper & Salt
Country of Origin: Spain
Breeder: Mr & Mrs Paradoms
Owner: Mrs K Wilberg
Sire: Pablo vd Ravenvennen
Dam: Isabell Von Der Edertalsperre

EXPLOSIV'S NIXON AT NIXADOR
DOB: 02/10/1987 Pepper & Salt
Country of Origin: Sweden
Breeder: Mrs L Carlstrom
Owner: Mrs T Jefferys
Sire: Explosiv's Macsimillian
Dam: Burston's Silver Fancy Free

VAN T WAREHEIM BIBA
DOB: 28/12/1986 Black
Country of Origin: South Africa
Breeder: Mr & Mrs J & E Gallant
Owner: Mr & Mrs R C Keable
Sire: S AFRICAN CH Iija vd Hohen Ward APT
Dam: S AFRICAN CH Wareheim Lothy APT

VAN T WAREHEIM QUEEN APT HDF
DOB: 19/01/1985 Black
Country of Origin: South Africa
Breeder: Mr & Mrs J & E Gallant
Owner: Mr & Mrs R C Keable
Sire: S AFRICAN CH Wareheim Feniks
Dam: Van T Gasey

PASSWORD V BERGHERBOS TO NENEVALE
DOB: 12/03/1989 ♂ Black
Country of Origin: Holland
Breeder: Mr J W Peters
Owner: Mrs J C Harrison-Smith
Sire: GERM CH Ray vd Hohen Ward Sch H III FH
Dam: NED CH Elle v Bergherbos

TINA
DOB: 12/10/1989 Black
Country of Origin: Poland
Breeder: Mr K Fus
Owner: Mr & Mrs Mikolajczak
Sire: POL CH Abar Kam-Bar-Negri
Dam: Dyna Tip Top

XEROS V BUCK OF NENEVALE
DOB: 12/10/1989 ♂ Black
Country of Origin: Germany
Breeder: R Dietsche-Lötscher
Owner: Mrs J C Harrison-Smith
Sire: NED CH Elzar v Bergherbos Wsg
Dam: GERM CH Nenevale Arina Kbsg Swiss Sgrn

XYLA V BUCK OF NENEVALE
DOB: 12/10/1989 ♀ Black
Country of Origin: Germany
Breeder: R Dietsche-Lötscher
Owner: Mrs J C Harrison-Smith
Sire: NED CH Elzar v Bergherbos Wsg
Dam: GERM CH Nenevale Arina Kbsg Swiss Sgrn

AM CH ZANTANAS GO FOR IT V YOULENE
DOB: 05/05/1986 ♂ Black
Country of Origin: Sweden
Breeder: Mr & Mrs Uddenholm
Owner: Mr & Mrs Krall
Sire: Zantanas Darth Weder Of Ifni
Dam: Zantanas Youlene

TRIUMPH VD NOORDERENK AT RILLATON
DOB: 04/06/1986 Black
Country of Origin: Holland
Breeder: Mr Liet
Owner: Mrs D Hounslow
Sire: Lars vd Noorderenk
Dam: Beries Flocsy

INKA DE PICHERA AT SANDRIDGE
♀

Country of Origin: Spain
Breeder: Giner Barat
Owner: Mr & Mrs J R Steele
Sire: SPAN CH Cunter De Better Can
Dam: Maat De Alevamiento De Pichera

STABLEMASTERS EX LEE
DOB: 30/09/1990 ♂ Black
Country of Origin: Finland
Breeder: Ms F Faberge
Owner: Mrs D Hounslow
Sire: CH Quintus v Bergherbos
Dam: Riesenhoff Ziggy-Twiggy

SKANSENS QUALITY AT ZANTANA
DOB: 15/08/1992 ♂
Country of Origin: USA
Breeder: Mrs S Hammarstrom
Owner: Mr & Mrs Krall
Sire: AM CH Raja De Pichera
Dam: AM CH Skansens Norah

SKANSENS QUALITY AT JAFRAK
DOB: 17/05/1992 ♀ Black
Country of Origin: USA
Breeder: Mrs S Hammarstrom
Owner: Mr & Mrs Krall
Sire: INT & AM CH Skansens Midnight Mozart
Dam: AM CH Mardi Gras

SKANSENS RUGBY AT JANNEM

Country of Origin: USA
Breeder: Mrs S Hammarstrom
Owner: Mrs J Hakki
Sire: AM CH Sieger v Bergherbos
Dam: AM CH Skansens Once Upon A Time

DONJUAN DE PICHERA AT FOXWOOD
DOB: 12/12/1993 ♂ Black
Country of Origin: Spain
Breeder: Giner Barat
Owner: Mr & Mrs Rylance
Sire: Uhlan De Pichera
Dam: SPAN & INT CH Zarza De Pichera

SKANSENS TORTELLINI AT JAFRAK
DOB: 05/10/1995 ♂ Black
Country of Origin: USA
Breeder: Mrs S Hammarstrom
Owner: Mr & Mrs Krall
Sire: AM CH Lucas De Campos De Oro
Dam: Skansens Swedish Summer

DONA TRUCHAS JUNIORDE LOS CHAPULITOS
DOB: 19/03/1995 ♀ Black
Country of Origin: Spain
Breeder: Mr R G Quiroga
Owner: Mr A Alvarez-Campos & Mrs J Alvarez-Kefford
Sire: Axcel De Campos De Oro
Dam: Anastasia De Espapanda

NERO DE NICKLAUSBRUNN
DOB: 09/11/1997 ♂ Pepper & Salt
Country of Origin: France
Breeder: Mr L Keller
Owner: Mr & Mrs D & C Loubignac
Sire: Skansen's Robert Redford
Dam: Giant Power's Just Daydream

SKANSENS WESTERN COWBOY AT JAFRAK
DOB: 06/03/1998 ♂ Black
Country of Origin: USA
Breeder: Ms S Hammarstrom
Owner: Mrs F Krall
Sire: AM CH Lucas De Campos De Ora
Dam: AM CH Skansens Salome

Photo at 11 months

HASSANHILL'S JOHN PLAYER SPECIAL
DOB: 28/01/1998 ♂ Black
Country of Origin: Sweden
Breeder: Mr & Mrs B & C Skalin
Owner: Mesdames J C Harrison-Smith & S J Hattrell-Brown
Sire: Swed & Nor CH Hassanhill's Hugo Boss
Dam: Catechism Ris'n Shine To Hassanhill

SKANSEN'S V I P SHIRALEE AT BELLGARD
DOB: 24/09/1997 ♀ Pepper & Salt
Country of Origin: USA
Breeder: Ms S Hammarstrom
Owner: Mr R Joy
Sire: AM CH Skansen's Union Jack
Dam: Skansen's Rainbow Special

STABLEMASTER'S BLONDE OF LEEBAY
DOB: 08/08/1994 ♀ Black
Country of Origin: Finland
Breeder: Ms F Faberge
Owner: Mrs B M Cocks
Sire: Stablemaster's Superman
Dam: Stablemaster's Dream of Glory

STABLEMASTER'S SEVENTH HEAVEN OF LEEBAY
DOB: 21/11/1995 ♀ Black
Country of Origin: Finland
Breeder: Ms F Faberge
Owner: Mrs B M Cocks
Sire: Span CH & INT Friper De Pichera
Dam: Stablemaster's Electric Lady

FANTASY DE LORDSHIP'S AT RIESENHEIM
DOB: 01/05/1999 ♀ Black
Country of Origin: Spain
Breeder: Luis Llin Talavera
Owner: Mr K J Rofe-Moss
Sire: Lennox-Lewis De Lordship's
Dam: Tequilla De Lordship's

FOREMAN DE LORDSHIP'S AT RIESENHEIM
DOB: 01/05/1999 ♂ Black
Country of Origin: Spain
Breeder: Luis Llin Talavera
Owner: Mr K J Rofe-Moss
Sire: Lennox-Lewis De Lordship's
Dam: Tequilla De Lordship's

SKANSEN'S KOIRA OF KELCANRICK

DOB: 22/12/1998 ♀ Pepper & Salt
Country of Origin: USA
Breeder: Mrs S Hammarstrom
Owner: Mrs R Rickard
Sire: AM CH Skansen's Union Jack
Dam: Skansen's Taboo

SKANSENS YANKEE CLIPPER AT JAFRAK

DOB: 22/05/2000 ♂ Black
Country of Origin: USA
Breeder: Mrs S Hammarstrom
Owner: Mr & Mrs Krall
Sire: Gloris Best Choice
Dam: Skansens Windstar

SKANSENS YESTERDAYS NEWS AT JAFRAK

DOB: 28/05/2000 ♂ Pepper & Salt
Country of Origin: USA
Breeder: Mrs S Hammarstrom
Owner: Mr & Mrs Krall
Sire: CH Tangamangas Rey Godo
Dam: Skansens Worthwhile

TOP-STYLE MUSTANG OF LEEBAY

DOB: 12/06/2000 ♂ Black
Country of Origin: Finland
Breeder: Mrs E Hakkinen
Owner: Mrs B M Cocks
Sire: Panomaks Alfa Romeo
Dam: Top-Style Loviatar

HASSANHILLS KNOWING ABOUT NENEVALE
DOB: 29/07/1998 ♀ Black
Country of Origin: Sweden
Breeder: Mr & Mrs B & C Skalin
Owner: Mrs J C Harrison-Smith
Sire: CH Leon della Selvafosca
Dam: Hassanhills Heaven or Hell

INT CH GLORIS IVAN IVANOVICH AT FOXWOOD
DOB: 23/10/1995 ♂ Black
Country of Origin: Russia
Breeder: Mrs O Seliverstova
Owner: Ms N Rylance & Mr & Mrs Moore
Sire: CH Zico De Campos De Oro
Dam: MULTI CH Stablemaster's Special Case

MONTE NEGRO SABOS KARALIENE OF LEEBAY
DOB: 25/05/2001 ♂ Black
Country of Origin: Lithuania
Breeder: G Naujakuriu
Owner: Mrs B M Cocks
Sire: Stablemaster's Bonaparte
Dam: Overheart

SASVARI NICOLE
DOB: 04/09/1998 ♀ Black
Country of Origin: Hungary
Breeder: Mrs A Vadocz
Owner: Mrs S Connett
Sire: Malya Kabul-N
Dam: Richesse Du Duc La Elzenhagen

TRINA VOM MOISBURGER BERG AT LEADENPENNY
DOB: 29/11/1999 ♀ Pepper & Salt
Country of Origin: Germany
Breeder: Mr R Forste
Owner: Mrs E Lewis-Cracknell
Sire: Germ CH Silver Senator Lamark
Dam: Jula Vom Moisburger Berg

DIAMBI NYUPHAI V WINRIKS HOF OF RILLATON
DOB: 14/05/2002 ♀ Pepper & Salt
Country of Origin: Netherlands
Breeder: Miss V D Honert
Owner: Mrs D Hounslow
Sire: Phaidon V Winriks Hof
Dam: Nyuka V Winriks Hof

HASSANHILL'S QUORUM FOR FERNCLIFFE
DOB: 06/05/2003 ♂ Black
Country of Origin: Sweden
Breeder: Mr & Mrs C & B Skalin
Owner: Mr K Carroll
Sire: Leon Della Selvafosca
Dam: Hassanhill's Lily Of The Valley

TYCHO NYUPHAI V WINRIKS HOF OF RILLATON
DOB: 14/05/2002 ♂ Pepper & Salt
Country of Origin: Netherlands
Breeder: Miss V D Honert
Owner: Mrs D Hounslow
Sire: Phaidon V Winriks Hof
Dam: Nyuka V Winriks Hof

NYUKA V WINRIKS HOF
DOB: 06/12/1999 ♀ Pepper & Salt
Country of Origin: Netherlands
Breeder: Miss A Van Den Honert
Owner: Mrs D Hounslow
Sire: Ned CH Icus V Winriks Hof
Dam: Rillaton Finality

HISTYLE'S FIRST LADY AT BELLGARD
DOB: 15/07/2004 ♀ Black
Country of Origin: USA
Breeder: Mr M & Mrs S Rutkas
Owner: Messrs R Joy & A Lightfoot
Sire: AM CH Histyle's Crusade
Dam: Histyle's Marquee

HISTYLE'S VANITY FAIR AT BELLGARD
DOB: 16/08/2004 ♀ Black
Country of Origin: USA
Breeder: Mr M & Mrs S Rutkas
Owner: Mr R Joy & Mr & Mrs K & S Cullen
Sire: Am Ch Gloris R Wiseguy Keystone
Dam: Histyle Dark Phoenix

KESHIA NYUPHAI V WINRIKS HOF
DOB: 14/05/2002 ♀ Pepper & Salt
Country of Origin: Netherlands
Breeder: Miss A Van Den Honert
Owner: Mrs D Hounslow
Sire: Phaidon V Winriks Hof
Dam: Nyuka V Winriks Hof

SKANSEN'S CAUGHT IN THE AFTERNOON WITH JAFRAK
DOB: 22/03/2004 ♀ Black
Country of Origin: USA
Breeder: Mrs S Hammarstrom
Owner: Mr & Mrs J Krall
Sire: AM CH Skansen's Youngblood
Dam: Skansen's Afternoon Delight

CON AMORE DA FELMOR TO COLDNOSE
DOB: 05/06/2004 ♂ Black
Country of Origin: Italy
Breeder: Mr L Bertini
Owner: Mrs J Lunn
Sire: CH Savali Bodyguard Zovely-N
Dam: CH Luna-N Degli Ussari Neri

RUS ASTERSHVARC REVOLUTION AT RIESENHEIM
DOB: 11/05/2005 ♂ Black
Country of Origin: Russian Federation
Breeder: Mrs O Grishina
Owner: Mr K J Rofe-Moss
Sire: Rus Grand CH Rus Astershvarc Yudgin
Dam: Rus CH Rus Astershvarc De Lux

SCAPMAN'S VALARAUKAR VON DASERBE
DOB: 02/12/2004 ♂ Black
Country of Origin: France
Breeder: Ms O Kerkela & Mr T Marquett
Owner: Mrs J T George
Sire: Span CH Greco De Pichera
Dam: FR & LUX CH Sloane De L'Ecurie De Syltemps

GENTLY BORN MOLOTOV AT FOXWOOD
DOB: 03/05/2005 ♂ Black
Country of Origin: Russia
Breeder: Mrs A Vlasova
Owner: Ms N Rylance & Mr & Mrs Moore
Sire: INT CH Gently Born Lexus
Dam: CH Gently Born Everlasting Love

SASVARI OLYMPIA FROM BLUEDANUBE
DOB: 28/11/2004 ♀ Black
Country of Origin: Hungary
Breeder: Dr E Vadocz
Owner: Mrs S Connett
Sire: Fekete Kraton Zsombor
Dam: Sasvari Blackberry

SASVARI ORIANA FROM BLUEDANUBE
DOB: 28/11/2004 ♀ Black
Country of Origin: Hungary
Breeder: Dr E Vadocz
Owner: Mrs S Connett
Sire: Fekete Kraton Zsombor
Dam: Sasvari Blackberry

BONY Z BEDYNKY MIT ZAUBER
DOB: 30/09/2004 ♀ Black
Country of Origin: Czech Republic
Breeder: Ms F Blatonova
Owner: Mr M G Hardy
Sire: FCI INT POL GERM CH Dies Irae Nergal
Dam: Iris Bitt Box

SKANSEN'S KODA OF KELCANRICK
DOB: 25/11/2005 ♂ Pepper & Salt
Country of Origin: USA
Breeder: Mrs S Hammarstrom
Owner: Mrs R Rickard
Sire: Skansen's American President
Dam: AM CH Happy Holiday V Winriks Hof

TANGLEWOOD'S WAR DANCE II
DOB: 19/03/2007 ♂ Black
Country of Origin: America
Breeder: Mr E Fojtik & Mr C & Mrs J Erath
Owner: Mr & Mrs K Cullen, Mr E Fojtik & Mr R Joy
Sire: AM CH Tanglewood's Khochise
Dam: AM CH Tanglewood's Blazing Star

GENTLY BORN DARK ENCHANTRESS OF DRAXPARK
DOB: 01/06/2007 ♀ Black
Country of Origin: Russian Federation
Breeder: Mrs A Vlasova & Trofimova
Owner: Mrs L J Parker
Sire: INT CH Gently Born Lexus
Dam: CH Gently Born Jolie Dominique

GUINNESS DE VENTACAN
DOB: 11/01/2004 ♂ Black
Country of Origin: Spain
Breeder: Mr A Castillo Rangel
Owner: Miss V Pass & Mr G Hitchin
Sire: SPAN CH Sultan De Ventacan
Dam: Lucy-Wills De Lordship's

HERR RIESEN QUEEN

DOB: 02/01/2007 ♀ Black
Country of Origin: Spain
Breeder: Mr A Sarciat
Owner: Mr K M & Mrs J Chamberlain
Sire: Dgentli Bon Clinton
Dam: Invicta Call Me Contraddiction-N

DRUMINPHILIPS ALIDA FOR FERNCLIFFE

DOB: 25/11/2007 ♀ Black
Country of Origin: Republic of Ireland
Breeder: Mrs S Freuhauf
Owner: Mrs K A Carroll
Sire: Elix Vom Schweigermoos
Dam: Kokapu Volgyi Otilia

DRUMINPHILIPS ASTERIX FOR FERNCLIFFE

DOB: 25/11/2007 ♂ Black
Country of Origin: Republic of Ireland
Breeder: Mrs S Freuhauf
Owner: Mrs K A Carroll
Sire: Elix Vom Schweigermoos
Dam: Kokapu Volgyi Otilia

FCI INT CH SAVALI LEVEL HI-FI AT FERNCLIFFE

DOB: 29/05/2003 ♂ Black
Country of Origin: Ukraine
Breeder: Ms S Oksana
Owner: Mr R A Latour
Sire: INT AM RUS EST CH Gloris Arizona Bill
Dam: RUS CH Odessa

MINT FLOWER Z TARTAKU WITH FOSTERGIANTS
DOB: 05/10/2007 ♀ Black
Country of Origin: Poland
Breeder: Mrs J Frycze
Owner: Mr A Galbraith
Sire: Refrain Brand New
Dam: POL CH Gloris Raspberry Jam

VENUS DE VENTACAN AT FOXWOOD
DOB: 01/10/2002 ♀ Black
Country of Origin: Spain
Breeder: Mr A Castillo
Owner: Miss V Pass & Mr G Hitchin
Sire: SPAN CH Sultan De Ventacan
Dam: Gatty De Pichera

CARAVAGGIO VOM MOISBURGER BERG AT LEADENPENNY
DOB: 01/01/2008 ♂ Pepper & Salt
Country of Origin: Germany
Breeder: Mr R Förste
Owner: Mrs E Lewis-Cracknell
Sire: Silver Senator Quintus
Dam: Amsel vom Moisburger Berg

RIANNA VON ELBERFELD
DOB: 01/11/2007 ♀ Black
Country of Origin: Germany
Breeder: Mrs M Moorman
Owner: Mr T Carter
Sire: Ferro V Elberfeld
Dam: Bille V Elberfeld

RISING SUN VON DER TALMUHLE

DOB: 21/02/2007 ♀ Black
Country of Origin: Germany
Breeder: Mr G Weilbacher
Owner: Mrs J T George
Sire: Ambros Von Der Talmuhle
Dam: Xanadu Von Der Talmuhle

UNBRIDLED DREAMS VOM HELLA-HOF

DOB: 06/12/2008 ♂ Black
Country of Origin: Germany
Breeder: T & S Hanze
Owner: Mr RG and Mrs SE Jackson
Sire: Faun Nergal
Dam: Kassiopeia vom Hella-Hof

SILVERSAGA'S DOLCE E GABBANA FOR LUCAVALE

DOB: 24/10/2008 ♂ Pepper & Salt
Country of Origin: Portugal
Breeder: Mr R P P Martins
Owner: Mr J M D Conway
Sire: Port CH Sascha De Romaniere
Dam: X-Extreme Beauty Z Grodu Ksiazat Pomorkish

YVES SAINT LAURENT VOM MEPHISTOPHELES AT FOXWOOD

DOB: 22/10/2009 ♂ Black
Country of Origin: Germany
Breeder: Ursula Römer-Goos
Owner: Mrs N Rylance
Sire: Mad Max z Tartaku
Dam: Atlantis vom Tornado

Evolution of the Giant Schnauzer on the European Continent
By Javier Sánchez (Barba Negra - Spain)

In the last 30 years dogs have had an unimaginable evolution for those that created the breed in the beginning. The character and appearance of our dogs has changed, influenced by better living conditions, the dog food that exits today, and the fact that the majority of breeds can no longer do the work for which they were created. There has been a logical and natural adaptation to the environment and contemporary life. Their greatest achievement, on the other hand, is the companion they have become at our side, and the extensive social network that has developed around the dog. People travel, meet up with friends and do sports with their dogs all with a common interest and love of the breed. The dogs can no longer take care of us as they did in the beginning. We have to take care of them.

The political changes in the European Continent along with the collapse of the Soviet Union have also had a major effect on the international map of dog breeding. Thousands and thousands of breeders and talented judges from many of the central and Eastern European countries have joined forces to organise dog breeding. For someone like me, whose origins and deep roots were motivated, by good luck, in the United Kingdom, all of these changing events have collided head-on against my conservative views regarding dog breeding.

Javier Sánchez with Erik de Barba Negra (9 months) in Oxford 1988
Owned by Mr & Mrs Wilberg

The massive increase in the breeding of pedigree dogs, as a way of life, has multiplied and exaggerated the number of specimens, but frequently it can be observed that it is to the detriment of quality. One of the problems is indeed that the newly emerging breeders did not have the opportunity to know the great dogs that have been famous in the breed. They only know those of today, and think the breed should be this way. It is not difficult to see today in the show ring, adult male Giants, moving happily with a wagging tail while watching his handler and awaiting a treat, really with the attitude of a Cocker Spaniel.

The Giant Schnauzer was born as a hard working dog, made of stone and not porcelain, as so many are seen today, they had a robust health and required only minimal and quick grooming. The current excess undercoat, the loss of quality and durability of the top coat, the endless hours of "grooming" with products and hair dryers are an affront to the pride of the breed, and unfortunately we can see this at almost every continental dog show.

Spain had two glorious decades, of which I am proud to have set off. During the eighties and nineties, the Spanish breeders were unbeatable. We were all young and we deployed a great amount of energy, travelling to all countries, accumulating the most important titles and raising excellent dogs, thanks to the fact we had party to an excellent gene pool.

Italy, with an old and serious tradition in the breed, France, and also Holland competed with rigor in the international scene. In Germany, the breeds country of origin, though not given to compete internationally, the Spaniards frequently won, even against the existing historical breeding affixes such as Gunterstal and Graifensie from which we started in the early days in Spain.

Ch Conny vd Hohen Ward
Ch Elmo vd Hohen Ward
The first Giants imported from Germany to Spain at the end of the 70's with Javier Sánchez

Finland also featured strongly with a couple of breeders, starting from the time the Government lifted the quarantine restrictions for dogs, and finally Russia in the late nineties. A country in which after a process of mass rearing at the hands of many people, are left with a small but active number of breeders, that if very prolific, especially two of them. The talent and the aggression of the Russians to "conquer" other countries with their dogs, has been and is so far unstoppable (although in Russia it is not prohibited to crop the ears and dock tails, it is not so practical for selling to other countries).

Currently, you almost never see a Giant Schnauzer win their respective group in a show on the continent. I visit shows every week but do not remember seeing this for a long time. Years ago this happened frequently and can be considered an indicator of the quality of the breed.

The Giant Schnauzer is not difficult to raise as other breeds, where two plus two rarely equals four, and it makes no major negative surprises. But mass breeding for a sufficiently long enough time has been incompatible with their purity and authenticity. It is not a pessimistic position but it is critical and realist. I'm counting that many people know this although nobody says it. It takes breeders who are less concerned with the economic benefit of breeding, and more who are serious and able to study and reflect a lot on what should be done before doing so. But without having the dogs of the past as an authentic reference point, it is not so easy.

My last Black Giant CH Pia von Gunterstal
She died at 17 years of age and never went to the vet

Choosing a Giant Schnauzer

Giant Schnauzers may live up to 12 years or more, they are a large and active breed that will take up a large part of your home and life in general. They need plenty of exercise as an adult and lots of guidance as a youngster. A good sense of humour on the part of the owner is essential along with firmness, fairness and consistency.

Giants are big characters and lots of fun, however their size and energy levels may not fit everyone's circumstances. Therefore if you are choosing a Giant Schnauzer it is better to do your research from the outset. And be warned, once you have decided to own a Giant, they can become addictive!

Is a Giant Schnauzer the Right Breed for You

Size

Giant Schnauzers are classed as a large breed, despite their name they are not actually a giant breed. However they are the Giant size of the three Schnauzer families. Males stand between 65-70 cms (25½ - 27½ inches) to the top of the shoulders and females 60-65 cms (23½ - 25½ inches). They can weigh between around 32kg (5 stones) for a small female and up to 55kg (8½ stones) for a large male. They are muscular and well boned, with a very large skull, big paws and a long and very 'waggy' tail.

Exercise

Adult Giants will require vigorous daily exercise with free running and mental stimulation. A good run twice a day should maintain a happy Giant, otherwise if left without the obligatory exercise or stimulation a Giant Schnauzer may become boisterous, and generally let you know they have energy to disperse.

During puppy-hood (up to 12 months) the amount of exercise needs to be limited in order to allow the puppy's joints to develop correctly. Free running exercise in an enclosed garden is best. In this way the puppy can rest when tired. Walking a puppy on a lead is fine but should be restricted initially, because the puppy cannot stop when they have done enough. On the other hand be prepared to physically prevent a puppy from overdoing free running exercise. Giant puppies can have a tendency to keep going until told to rest.

Grooming

Giants are a trimmed breed, they do not tend to shed their coat, and will require regular weekly brushing and combing, especially the longer beard and furnishings. Professional trimming will be required regularly depending on the type of coat; approximately every 2 months if the coat has a tendency to be soft, and approximately every 3-4 months for the correct harsh coat. Without regular trimming they will loose their characteristic expression and outline.

Training

Being an intelligent breed, Giants do very well with obedience training. They are quick to learn but can sometimes have a slight stubborn streak, which is thought to be linked to their intelligence. Giants respond best to short training sessions with positive feedback in the form of treats, toys and fun.

Puppies will require training and socialising from a very early age in order to learn the ground rules and basic manners. Also since the breed can be slow to mature mentally they will need consistent guidance from puppy through to adolescence.

Family Compatibility

Giants are a 'people' breed, they are loyal and devoted to their family. They need to be with people and will keep a close eye on your whereabouts at all times, they will constantly be near your side no matter what. Their boundless energy makes them excellent play mates for older children. However, since they are strong and agile they could unintentionally knock over a small toddler during play, and therefore require supervision around young children.

General Breed Traits

Giant Schnauzers were originally bred to herd and guard cattle and watch over the farmstead. They have natural guard and watchful instincts, and as such will bark when a stranger approaches the home. In the absence of dominant peers the Giant may assume the position of dominance. Therefore firmness, fairness and consistency are necessary to ensure they remain as a subordinate member of the family. Giants are a bold, reliable and versatile breed making them adaptable to many activities from family companion to obedience, agility, working trials and generally anything that is fun.

Where to Find More Information

The Giant Schnauzer Club organise a breed stand at the annual Discover Dogs event usually held at Earls Court each November, and also every year at Crufts in March. The Discover Dogs stand provides first hand information to the public regarding everything, and anything, related to Giant Schnauzer ownership. The stand is manned by experienced Giant owners and provides an opportunity to meet the dogs and speak to their owner or breeder.

The Giant Schnauzer Club also offers an annual seminar, either a grooming workshop, in which Giant owners receive grooming tuition and any advice regarding care of their dog. Alternatively, hands on assessments are provided, where anyone interested in the breed or those wishing to progress towards judging can learn more about conformation and movement.

The Club also holds a list of breeders that are members who agree to abide by the rules and regulations of the Club along with its code of ethics. The list of breeders is published via the website and available from the Club Secretary. Many of these breeders are happy to chat and freely provide information about the breed. Responsible breeders will also be willing to allow prospective new owners to visit and meet their dogs and discuss the characteristics and requirements of the breed.

Puppy or Rescue/Re-home?

There are a number of advantages and disadvantages when considering a puppy compared to an older dog in need of a new home.

Dogs requiring re-homing are generally older or young adults having already gone through the puppy chewing/teething and house training stage, also they are normally happy to be placed in a loving home. Some, however, may have been neglected and require patience and care to facilitate the transition between homes.

A rescue dog will have had at least one home and may, or may not, have already developed bad habits, or problems due to the fact that they may have been rejected. In comparison a puppy's behaviour can be shaped from the very beginning, although puppy training will require time, patience and perseverance. Rearing a puppy is often compared to bringing up a baby, not only in the amount of care required, but also for the emotional power of the experience.

Although there will be an initial adjustment period for both a puppy and a rescue/re-home, puppies will most likely require a prolonged period of input and socialisation for around the first 18 months. Whereas with a rescue/re-home, once past the first few months, the dog learns to depend on the kindness of his new owners, and they often settle quickly and forge a bond. Providing a loving, home for a dog in need, can often be very rewarding, although sometimes difficult, initially. The dog may need to learn to trust again, or even for the first time. Separation anxiety, fear of noises, and attempts to run away are possibilities.

Nevertheless, the puppy or older Giant can provide a loyal and devoted companion, the choice is down to individual preference and circumstances.

Male or Female?

Although all Giant Schnauzers possess the characteristics of the breed, each has their own individual personality independent of whether they are male or female. Some males may be very laid back, others more dominant, some may be very active and others more passive, likewise for females. Therefore the decision between a male or female in some respects can be quite subjective. It is always better to see the parents where possible, and speak to the breeder about the temperament of the relevant breeding lines.

The most obvious issue regarding a male or female is their size. Males are generally of a much larger stature, stronger and more powerful. There is also a hormonal factor requiring consideration. Females will have an oestrus cycle every 6-8 months, where the bitch will be in season for around 3 weeks. During this time segregation will be required to prevent unwanted pregnancies. Giant Schnauzer females may also have a tendency towards phantom pregnancies. Males can also become hormonal and mark their territory, seek out bitches in season and display mounting or dominant behaviour. However spaying or castration is an option available to prevent unwanted puppies and also in the management of some hormone related behaviours.

The existence of other dogs in the household is also another consideration, as some Giant males may not co-habit amicably with another male, similarly with two females. Again it is important to talk to the breeder as they will be most knowledgeable regarding individual temperaments and co-habiting potential.

Whether choosing a male or female, training is essential for the dog to be a valuable part of the family. Dogs have to be taught what is expected of them, just like children. Behaviours that show dominance or aggression may be altered with training. Because dogs are pack animals, they need to know their place in the pack. Until they learn their place, they may test you or your family members to see exactly who is the leader of the pack.

Finding a Breeder

When looking for a healthy and well adjusted Giant Schnauzer puppy it is the breeder that is the most important consideration.

It is better to avoid buying a puppy that is either going 'cheap', from a pet shop, or handed over on premises such as a car park, as there is every possibility that the pup may be from a disreputable source. Getting a puppy from a responsible breeder can increase the chances that the dog will live a happy and healthy life. The Giant Schnauzer Club hold a list of breeders who are members of the Club, and as such agree to adhere to the code of ethics regarding the welfare and breeding of dogs. However the Club cannot endorse or guarantee any particular breeder.

What to Expect From a Responsible Breeder

- A responsible breeder will plan litters in advance.

- The breeder should be able to provide knowledgeable information regarding the characteristics and suitability of the breed.

- The breeder will ask questions regarding your home/family circumstances.

- Provide an opportunity to meet the dam, and wherever possible the sire and any other relatives. This will give you a better idea of the likely temperament, type and size of the puppy.

- Provide an opportunity to see the environment in which the puppies have been raised, and observe how the litter interact where possible.

- Assess the puppy's temperament and give guidance to new owners when choosing an appropriate puppy best suited to individual circumstances.

- Written information on feeding, flea and worming treatment, exercise, training, socialisation, training and general care.

- Information about any immunisations that may have been administered and requirements for any further vaccinations.

- A signed puppy sales contract outlining any endorsements which may have been placed on the puppy, and also any terms and conditions and/or requirements of the breeder and new owner.

- A copy of the pedigree.

- Just like humans, some breeds of dogs can be affected by inherited conditions. The Kennel Club and the British Veterinary Association currently offer the BVA/KC/ISDS eye scheme relevant to the Giant Schnauzer, which aims to detect and monitor Hereditary Cataracts (HC) within the breed. The eye scheme is also currently available as an option to monitor Multifocal Retinal Dysplasia (MRD) in puppies' eyes between 6 and 12 weeks. And the BVA/KC hip scheme is also available for breeders wishing to reduce the risk and/or monitor Hip Dysplasia. The breeder should provide copies of the current eye certificates for the sire and the dam, litter eye screening form and any other relevant health test results that may have been undertaken.

- Encourage new owners to attend training/obedience classes.

- Encourage new owners to join a Schnauzer specific breed club.

- Puppies advertised as being Kennel Club registered should be registered by the breeder and the KC certificate handed over at the time of purchase or very soon after.

- Provide transfer of ownership information and signature from the breeder allowing the registration to be transferred.

- Provide a practical level of after care advice and information.

- Accept a level of responsibility should a puppy/adult require re-homing.

The Kennel Club Accredited Breeder Scheme

THE KENNEL CLUB

ACCREDITED BREEDER SCHEME

Responsible dog ownership is a top priority for the Kennel Club, and through the Accredited Breeder Scheme it helps both breeders and prospective puppy buyers to maintain their responsibilities in terms of dogs' health and vitality.

Established in 2004 the Accredited Breeder Scheme is a voluntary scheme which is open to all breeders - both large and small - who are willing to follow the basic requirements of responsible breeding. Most scheme members breed infrequently, having just one litter a year. Those who breed more frequently can still become members providing that they adopt similar principles and good practice.

Many prospective puppy buyers contact the Kennel Club for advice on finding and buying a puppy. In response to these enquiries the Kennel Club provides a free list of all Accredited Breeders for the relevant breed plus access to an online 'Find a Puppy' service. Any breeder may pay to advertise their registered litters on the 'Find a Puppy' service, but Accredited Breeder litters will be flagged and will always appear at the top of the list.

Becoming an Accredited Breeder
There are ten set requirements that Accredited Breeders must agree to follow, which encourage the breeding of healthy, well-adjusted puppies. In return the breeder will be able to use the scheme literature and log to promote litters.

Annual membership entitles you to use the online Kennel Club Puppy Sales Register - www.findapuppy.org.uk - free of charge and will highlight your litter to puppy buyers as being bred by an Accredited Breeder. You will also gain prioritised access to additional advice and information from the Kennel Club's Health and Breeder Services Department.

The Scheme joining fee is £15 and annual renewal is £10. The joining fee includes a certificate, a pack of scheme leaflets and ten Puppy Sales Wallets.

An Accredited Breeder must:

- Ensure that all breeding stock is Kennel Club registered and take all reasonable steps to ensure that it is healthy and able to function normally (fit for function: fit for life).

- Hand over the dog's registration certificate at time of sale if available, or forward it to the new owner as soon as possible. Explain any endorsements that might pertain and obtain written and signed confirmation from the new owner, at or before the date on which the dog is physically transferred, that the new owner is aware of the endorsement(s), regardless of whether or not the endorsed registration certificate is available.

- Follow Kennel Club policy regarding maximum age and number/frequency of litters.

- Permanently identify breeding stock by DNA profile, microchip, or tattoo.

- Make use of Kennel Club health screening schemes, relevant to their breed, on all breeding stock. These schemes include DNA testing, hip dysplasia, elbow dysplasia and inherited eye conditions.
- Give written, breed-specific advice in the Puppy Sales Wallet on:
  - Tendencies or potential traits in the breed
  - Socialization, exercise and training
  - Feeding and worming programmes
  - Grooming
- Provide a written record, in the Puppy Sales Wallet, on the immunisation measures taken.
- Provide reasonable post-sales telephone advice and endeavour to deal with any issues arising in good faith.
- Inform buyers of the requirements and the recommendations that apply to Kennel Club Accredited Breeders as well as the existence of the complaints procedure.
- Draw up a contract of sale for each puppy and provide a copy in the Puppy Sales Wallet.

In addition the scheme has a number of recommendations:

Kennel Club Accredited Breeders are strongly encouraged to:

- Make sure that whelping facilities meet with good practice.
- Follow any relevant breed specific recommendations.
- Ensure that the contract of sale clearly lays out to the buyer the nature and details of any guarantee given (e.g. time limit) and/or any provisions for refund or return and replacement of puppy. If endorsements are being used the contract should also explain why these have been placed and under what circumstances they would be removed (if any). The contract should be signed and dated by both breeder and purchaser, showing that both have agreed to these terms.
- Encourage new owners to take their puppy to the vet as soon as possible after taking delivery of it.
- Commit to help, if necessary, with the re-homing of a dog, for whatever reason, throughout the dog's lifetime.
- Participate in any breed health survey or other health initiatives in their breed.

Further details on how to join the Scheme can be found at:
www.thekennelclub.org.uk/accreditedbreederscheme
For further information please contact:
The Kennel Club Press Office
020 7518 1008
press.office@thekennelclub.org.uk
www.thekennelclub.org.uk

Dog Breeding Checklist
Copyright the Kennel Club
Reproduced with their permission

If you are contemplating dog breeding, there are certain questions that you will need to ask yourself before proceeding:

- Have I the time to devote to a litter until the puppies are old enough to go to their new homes, which is usually around eight weeks?
- Am I knowledgeable enough to advise new owners about the various aspects of caring for their puppies, including rearing, diet, training and health problems? Can I afford to pay for the recommended health tests for the bitch prior to mating her and, where necessary, her litter?
- Do I know enough to help the bitch during the whelping, if necessary?
- Can I afford to pay for a caesarean should the dam have difficulty whelping the litter?
- Could I cope with a very large litter of, say, 10 or 12 puppies?
- Do I have sufficient knowledge to rear the litter correctly, including on worming, vaccinations and socialisation?
- Would I be able to find good homes for the puppies?

Am I in a position to take back or re-home any puppies if it becomes necessary? If you have not been able to say yes to all of the above questions, then dog breeding may not be for you. You may therefore wish to consider having your bitch spayed to prevent unwanted or unplanned pregnancies; your breed club or the breeder of your bitch may be able to provide you with further expert advice.

If you have been able to say yes to all of the above questions, do not forget that you will also need to keep the following in mind:

- Responsible dog breeders believe that each litter that they breed, should be an improvement on the parents.
- Responsible dog breeders give careful consideration to health issues, temperament and soundness.
- Responsible dog breeders plan ahead of each mating so as to ensure that each puppy produced will be bred in the best possible environment.
- Responsible dog breeders accept responsibility for a puppy which they have bred, and make themselves available to give advice, help and information to new owners.

Keeping Our Breed Healthy

The Giant Schnauzer Club has a fundamental duty of care for the health of the breed and as such encourages breeders and owners alike to participate in the Giant Schnauzer Club breed health plans:

1. Breed Health Survey
The Giant Schnauzer Club is working in collaboration with all four UK Schnauzer Clubs in relation to an ongoing and annual joint breed health survey. Results of the surveys are to be collated and published via the Giant Jottings club magazine and website.

2. KC/BSAVA Scientific Advisory Group
The Giant Schnauzer Club is in consultation with Professor Jeff Sampson the Kennel Club Geneticist and health representatives via the KC/BSAVA Scientific Advisory Group.

3. Animal Health Trust DNA Samples
The Giant Schnauzer Club would like to encourage owners of dogs affected with melanomas (cancer) of the skin, toe and mouth and also dogs diagnosed with Idiopathic (inherited) Epilepsy, to send cheek swab samples to the Animal Health Trust. It is hoped the samples will help to assist with future research in to genetic testing for melanomas in Schnauzers and Idiopathic Epilepsy in all dogs in general. The Animal Health Trust also requires cheek swab samples from unaffected dogs over the age of 7 years.

4. Data Collection
The Giant Schnauzer Club actively encourages owners and breeders of dogs affected with any inherited conditions to submit relevant veterinary information and supporting pedigrees for inclusion in the breed health file to enable real life data collection. It is more meaningful if such records contain specific notes on any investigations undertaken, so that it can be distinguished which dogs

have simply been reported as having symptoms from those that have had comprehensive clinical assessments and diagnosed with specific conditions.

5. Health Screening

The Giant Schnauzer Club recommends that, as minimum, breeders adhere to the required health screening tests relevant to the breed i.e. at the time of publication, eye testing for Hereditary Cataracts and litter screening puppies eyes for Multifocal Retinal Dysplasia (MRD). The BVA/KC Hip Dysplasia scheme is also available as an option for breeders to enable monitoring of Hip Scores within the breed.

Unfortunately the genetic position regarding many conditions currently remains unclear. There is a possibility that some health problems such as Hypothyroid, Epilepsy, and Melanomas may have an inherited link within the breed. However there are no conclusive answers as to the mode of inheritance for such conditions which can present a challenge to the breed and canine world in general. As such a collaborative and long term approach to minimising incidences of any health problem is required and real life data collection is key. In the interim the Giant Schnauzer Club recommend a common sense approach, in that breeders should avoid the mating of affected dogs and also avoid repeat matings that produced affected offspring. The health status of any breeding pair and their ancestry requires careful consideration.

Although the club can monitor and report on health trends within the breed, due to legal complexities of the Data Protection Act it would be inappropriate for the club to print individual names of dogs and their pedigrees.

Hopefully with the help of breeders, owners and advancements in research and technologies the future may provide more conclusive answers that will assist in keeping our breed as healthy as possible.

The Giant Schnauzer Club strongly recommends that:

- All adult breeding stock to be tested annually for life under the BVA/KC eye scheme.
- All puppies to be eye tested at 6-12 weeks i.e. prior to leaving the breeder, this test is for M.R.D not cataracts.
- All puppies registration documents to be endorsed R - progeny not eligible for Registration.
- Dogs attending for eye tests to be identified by microchip prior to testing (this does not yet apply to litter screening of pups under 12 weeks old).

Showing Your Giant Schnauzer
By Frances Krall

A Giant Schnauzer is a dog to be proud of; A dog with tremendous aesthetic appeal.

If you purchased your Giant from an established show kennel, the breeder will probably want you to show, and offer help and encouragement. You will need to learn the art of trimming your Giant for the show ring and of course keep him in good muscular condition. Showing your Giant can be a wonderful interest and hobby; you will meet people from all walks of life who share the interest with you, and friendships will be forged that will last your lifetime. It is necessary for a proviso to be added here. Showing you Giant can be fun provided you have the temperament for the sport! If your love and regard for your Giant will remain constant, regardless of success or failure in the show ring, then by all means enter the show world, share the pleasure of the day out with your Giant, rejoice in the wins and accept the losses. Remember you are showing for fun, there are no financial rewards - just a little prestige; a few red cards, or even a title, will not make your Giant a better companion or a truer friend. Showing is an expensive and time consuming hobby, and if you do get bitten by the show bug then the dog scene will become a way of life.

A great asset to those who wish to show their dog, is to learn to lose, preferably before you acquire the taste for winning.
To gain the odd prize card gives encouragement and spurs you on to greater ambition. Too much success too soon, although enjoyable at the time, denies you the benefits of the apprenticeship served over years of striving, coping with disappointments and hopefully, disregarding the rose-coloured spectacles which we all understandably, see our own much loved Giants.

If you have bred or bought a promising puppy with showing in mind and you have reared the pup to the very best of your ability, you will probably be longing to get your puppy into the show ring. I always advise that it is a long tiring day for a puppy at a show it is wise never to over show him, Giants are so bright they easily become bored and it will also affect their physical development.

Teaching the puppy to stand and trot for suitable lengths of time must be made enjoyable. Ask a friend to gently 'go over' the pup, to look at the teeth, to attract the puppy's attention and to generally persuade the pup that the judging process is pleasant. Local ring craft classes are invaluable, but again do not overdo it, you don't want to turn an interested baby into a showing robot.

Good handling is making your Giant look the very best, and to do that you need to understand your Giant's construction. You must know and maximise the virtues, and recognize and minimise the failings, you must study movement and find the optimum speed, and develop the knack of getting your Giant's attention in order to show some sparkle at the crucial time.

Another very important aspect of showing your Giant is learning the art of trimming, you can improve the looks of a mediocre specimen by clever trimming but you can also ruin the best specimen with bad trimming. To learn how to trim and to make the best of you Giant you must at first rely on the help of the breeder of your puppy, most are more than happy for you to visit regularly for help, but don't turn up at a show and expect them to work a miracle on a shaggy unkempt Giant at the last minute, for one thing they will be busy with their own dogs, and secondly grooming is an on going job and not all of it can be done at the last minute. The breed Clubs often run trimming workshops which are a great help, and when you are at shows watch the experienced handlers and groomers there is always something you can learn from them.

The Giant Schnauzer Club Open Show February 2007
Junior Handler Miss Hannah Houchin age 14 years winning BOB and RBIS

The Kennel Club and the GSC like to encourage young people to get involved in all aspects of dog showing.

Supreme Champion
Jafrak Philippe Olivier Phil

"Phil's favourite show was always Crufts,... he must have known 2008 was his last chance because he showed like he's never shown before."

How it all Began - by Sandie & Kevin Cullen

Who would have thought on that day in 1995 we went to collect our giant puppy from Jack and Frances Krall, it would change our lives forever.

Jake was a big beautiful boy. We were very proud to own this handsome boy but had no intention of showing him. We were happy with a good looking pet. Jake was such a clever puppy that we decided to take him to training classes. It turned out the training class we went to was actually ringcraft and not obedience at all. We stayed anyway and everybody at the class said what a beautiful dog we had and suggested that we show him. And that's where it all started.

We were all set for Jake's first show, very excited but a little scared. We never actually made it to the show because the day before Jake decided to scale our six foot garden fence and run into the oncoming traffic. He was nearly killed but he was such a strong dog he pulled through but had pins in his leg and couldn't be shown. Jake was only nine months when this happened but despite his injuries he still lived with us until he was thirteen and a half.

After all this we liked the idea of showing our dogs and went back to Jack and Frances for a show puppy. So Willow came to live with us (Jafrak Night on the Tiles). We showed Willow with some success but she really didn't like the show ring and ended up staying home with Jake. It became clear that Kevin had a natural talent with the handling and grooming and it was something we were not going to be able to stop.

By now we had the show bug and there's no cure so came Lola (Jafrak Dolcelata) and Samson (Jafrak Zucchini) litter brother and sister, who became our first two champions. Lola turned out to be very special, producing Philippe Olivier in her first litter, who we will talk about later. And Samson was a big winner taking Best of Breed at Crufts two years running, and taking group three one year. He was also top giant. He was also the sire of our next two champions, Leila (Jafrak Dream Come True) and Shadow (Jafrak Dream On). Next came Grace (Jafrak Brushstrokes) who is still today the bitch CC record holder with 25 CCs.

Now where do we start with Philip (Jafrak Philippe Olivier)?

Phil (left) at 7 weeks old with his sister Martina - Jafrak Lola Lasagne

When you are looking at an eight week old puppy running around your kitchen getting into mischief with the other dogs you would never dream that seven years down the line he would be a Crufts Supreme Champion. That's exactly what happened with Philip.
Phil won Best Puppy in Show at his first show. We knew he was a special dog but never knew how special he would actually be. He had his first CC, Best of Breed and went on to Best in Show at the Schnauzer Club of Great Britain, at eleven months old.

In 2003 he did what most people only dream of and won an all breed Best in Show. That was the most amazing day and we would never have believed that he would go on to win thirteen more.

In 2003 Phil was Top Dog, All Breeds.

Midland Counties 2007 one of Phil's 14 Best in Show wins

Phil's favourite show was always Crufts. He always seemed to know this was a special show and gave a fantastic performance, but he must have known 2008 was his last chance because he showed like he's never shown before. There was something about him that year, from the breed ring to the Best in Show line up, he was not going to be denied for a third time. He's always had an incredible rapport with Kevin, you can see they adore each other when they are in the ring, and that's what took them all the way to Best in Show. Something you never ever believe you could ever win but every exhibitor dreams of winning. We have had the most amazing time with Phil for which we thank him. He's a once in a lifetime dog.

Phil is now nine years old enjoying his daily walks with his grandchildren and great grandchildren who are starting to enjoy their time in the show ring.

We would like to thank Jack and Frances Krall for all these lovely dogs and the knowledge they have given us.

Giant Schnauzer Welfare
By Mrs H J Smith

What to Do If You Can No Longer Look After Your Giant

The Giant Schnauzer Club operates a Re homing and Rescue Service for any Giant which may need help. Owners may not be able to look after their Giant for a variety of reasons and, therefore, should, initially, get in touch with their breeder. Any responsible breeder will help with the re homing of their stock (as per KC Code of Ethics) at any stage of the Giants life. Fortunately, we do not have a huge rescue problem in Giants, as most breeders are responsible when selling their puppies and issue an agreement which stipulates that the owner contacts them should their circumstances change .If the breeder is unable to help, the GSC will be happy to re home the dog in conjunction with the owners. It would be in the best interests of the dog if the current owners could keep the dog until a suitable family could be selected from the waiting list, which the Club is in the very enviable position of having at the moment. Only in an emergency situation or in the case of an abandoned dog would the Giant be taken into the Rescue kennels. The Rescue Co-ordinator would ask a series of questions to be sure that the right decision had been made in what is, obviously, a difficult situation. These questions greatly help in putting the right new owners in touch with the current ones.

The Dogs That Come Into Re Home and Rescue

Many types of dog come into Re home but some can be a little more complicated than others. Young, dominant males can require a great amount of time, patience and training especially if, as a puppy, has been allowed to do what he wanted for the past 16 months or so.

Sometimes, an owner may be hospitalised or ill and have to unfortunately give up their beloved friend. A suitable home may be difficult to find for an older Giant for no other reason than their age. Abandoned Giants are, thankfully, rare and we know little about them or where they came from. In one case, an abandoned bitch was re homed and taken to the vets for routine spaying and, unfortunately, it was found she had a terminal illness. The question is, was she abandoned to avoid vets fees, we will never know. These owners have now gone on to re home another Giant through our Re home program. Thank goodness for people like this without whom we could not operate our service.

If You Can Re Home a Giant

If you think you could possibly give a Giant a home please contact the Rescue Co-ordinator of the GSC(see website) who will take your details and ask a variety of questions regarding the dog's potential new home. All new owners should be happy to be house checked at some point by the GSC. Sometimes we require an experienced home, but that is not always essential. It would be advisable to research the breed to be sure you know what is involved in taking on a Giant Schnauzer. Remember that it can take time for some dogs to settle in new surroundings, some needing extra TLC. Of course, don't forget a huge sense of humour is definitely a must, as a Giant will always make you smile! The GSC will give you a year's free membership, which will provide help and support. The Rescue Coordinator will always be there to help you overcome any problems or issues.

And Finally

The Club calls on many people to help operate our service and we would like to thank everyone involved. All the work is done voluntarily, but, of course, we incur costs, such as vet's fees, kennelling, travelling etc. For that reason we do ask for donations, without which we would not be able to function.

Remember, if you go to buy a Giant Schnauzer puppy: it does grow, it will be destructive, they will steal your food when you are not looking and they can knock small children over, they won't think they have done anything wrong! Training is essential from the very first day and, if so, you will be thoroughly rewarded with a well behaved pet. This puppy's welfare is essentially your responsibility .The breeder and the GSC will give you help every step of the way, should you need it.

If you do find that you really can no longer look after your Giant, for whatever reason, please call your breeder and the GSC. Don't put your dog on the internet for someone to profit from or place in an unsuitable home. We love our breed and we do our utmost to go that extra mile to protect it.

Grooming, Clipping and Trimming

Giant Schnauzers are a 'trimmed breed' with minimal shedding compared to short course coated breeds. Therefore the coat will require regular attention either by hand-stripping to remove dead hair or clipping. To keep a Giant Schnauzer with their typical Schnauzery look and expression they will need a visit to a groomer approximately every 8-12 weeks. Alternatively you may wish to learn how to groom yourself. It is important that puppies are trained to sit and stand on a table for grooming, even if you don't intend to do them yourself it will make the job easier for your groomer. You don't need to buy an expensive grooming table, any small, steady table covered with rubber matting, to prevent slipping, will be ideal. The coat and furnishings require brushing out and combing on a daily basis.

Strip Or Clip The Body Coat

Giant Schnauzers have a double coat, a waterproof course top coat and a downy undercoat. Depending on the type of coat, if left it will become 'blown' once or twice a year. The longer dead top coat becomes loose and puffed out with new coat and undercoat coming in underneath. Stripping is the removal of the long, dead hair either by hand or with the aid of a stripping knife. Stripping of the coat can be time consuming but it will maintain texture and is required for the show ring. If there is a great deal of undercoat, start by removing as much as possible by scraping the body with the serrated edge of the stripping knife.

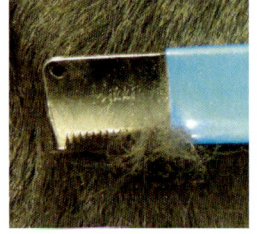

To strip the coat brush the hair backwards, and start at the base of the tail, with the stripping knife in the palm of your hand and the serrated edge down, pull out a few hairs by trapping them between your thumb and the knife blade, giving a sharp pull in the direction of coat growth. Work on a small area at a time leaving just the undercoat close to the skin.

Once stripped the faster growing undercoat can be maintained by regular scraping with the stripping knife. The frequency of scraping will depend on the abundance and growth rate of the undercoat, regular scraping may also help to improve a softer coat.

If you are not able to strip the body coat and if your dog is not being shown a clipped coat is a quicker and easier option. However clipping of the 'body coat' will cause the coat to lose its course texture and become much softer. Also clipping does not remove undercoat and the overall coat colour may appear duller.

Using a course stripping knife strip the coat within the dotted area and in the same direction the coat grows as shown.

If you prefer to clip your dog use blade No 7F

Continue stripping to the midline of the rear.

Clipping the Rear and Abdomen

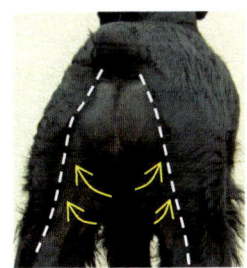

Using blade No 10 clip the rear and inner thigh to the natural hairline as shown.

N.B: Check the density of the hair in this area as a longer blade may be preferred.

Clip the dog's bottom across the thigh to the centre. Clip 1- 2 inches upwards on the underside of the tail.

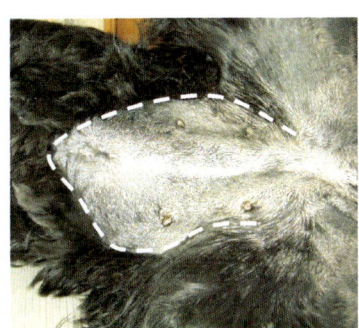

Continue clipping the abdomen up to the naval as shown.

Tail

Strip the upper and sides of the tail as per the body coat. Comb down the feathering underneath the tail and trim the underside, neaten the end of the tail into a blunt rounded end.

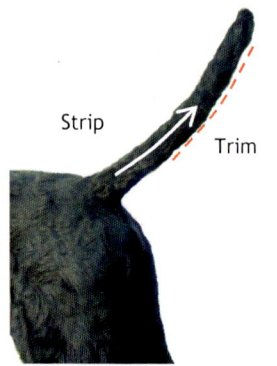

Alternatively the tail may be clipped off all over.

Head

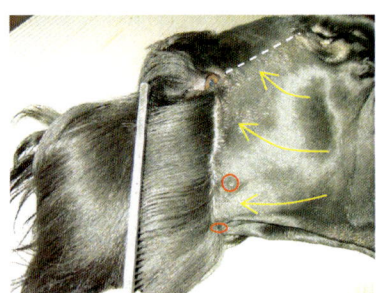

Using the large nodular whiskers (identified by red circles) as a guide, brush the beard away from the face. Clip with blade No10 in the direction show up to the ridge of the skull.

The hair between the eyes should form a diamond shape. Accentuate this line by scissoring from the corners of the eyes. Clean a small area out between the eyebrows with the clippers or scissors - keep the scissors 'flat' to the skull and this will prevent scissor marks.

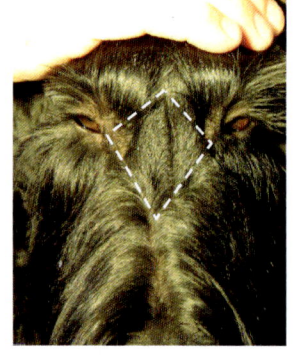

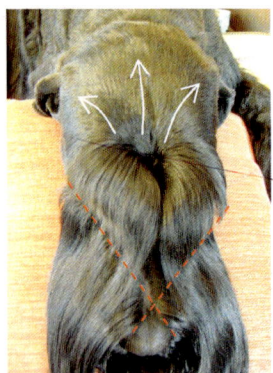

Trim the eyebrows in a line with the nose as shown. Strip the top of the head in the direction of the arrows with a fine stripping knife, alternatively clip with blade No 8 or 10. The beard will require regular washing and brushing with a slicker brush to remove knots and also combing through. The beard will only need trimming once every few years or so if it becomes too long.

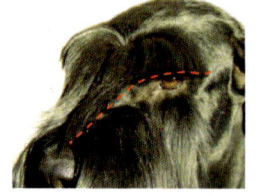

Neck and Chest

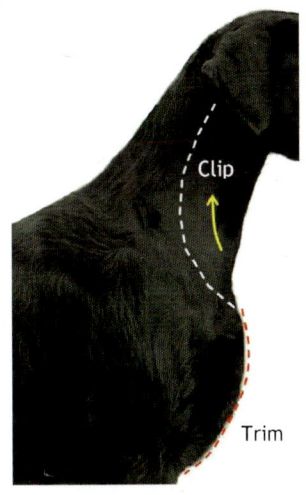

Continue clipping the throat and neck with blade No10 from behind the ears to the breast bone. Blend in with thinning scissors or by stripping.

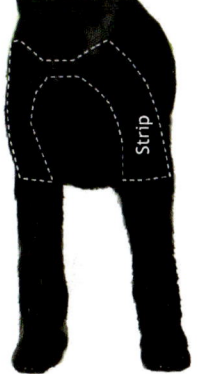

Strip or clip the front of the upper arms to blend in with the body

Trim and neaten the chest hair

Ears

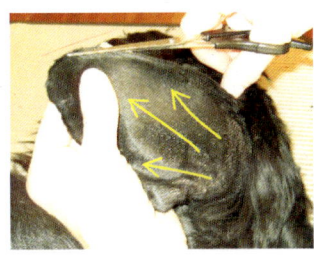

Clip the ears with blade No10 in the direction of the arrows.

Trim the edges of the ear with scissors to give a neat edge.

Keep the ears clean and free of wax by using an ear cleaning solution. Remove as much hair as possible from the inside of the ear canals by plucking out a few hairs at a time with flat-ended tweezers. An abundance of hairs inside the ear can lead to infection.

Feet

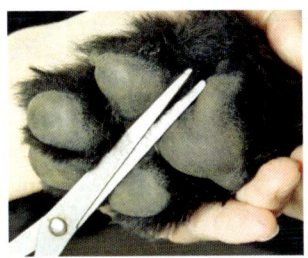

Trim the fur in-between the pads with scissors. This will prevent clogs of dirt and mats from causing sore feet.

With the dog standing up, trim the hair around each foot to create a round 'Cats Paw' effect.

Legs

The leg furnishings will need brushing regularly with a slicker brush and combing through to prevent mats from developing. The frequency of brushing/trimming will depend on the density and texture of the coat.

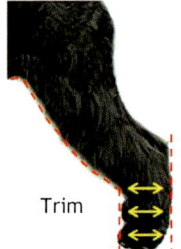
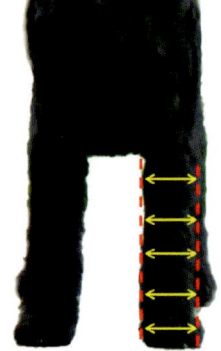

Trim the legs to keep them neat, comb the hair out as shown by the arrows and trim the leg hair straight all the way around each leg. Trim the back legs along the natural curve of the thigh.

Underline

Neaten the underline in a straight line in to the tuck up.

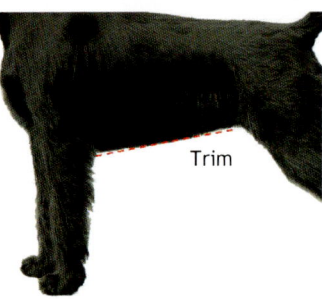

Teeth

Raw knuckle bones from the butcher are a great way to clean Giant Schnauzers teeth, and they love them! Do not give cooked bones as they may splinter and become lodged in the throat or gut. Canine denture sticks, and dental chew toys will also help to keep the teeth clean.

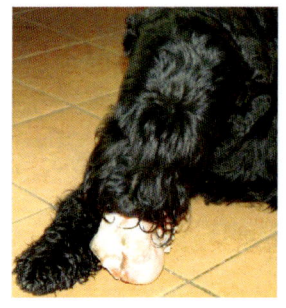

Inspect the teeth on a regular basis observing for any signs of tartar; a hard coating that builds up due to plaque. It is usually brown or yellow in colour.

Nails

Giant Schnauzers have very thick and dark nails, an electric nail grinder is ideal. Take off small amounts at a time to prevent trimming into the quick, which will cause bleeding. Check the length of the nails regularly, including dew claws if present. Exercising on a hard surface will also help to file the nails.

Grooming Equipment

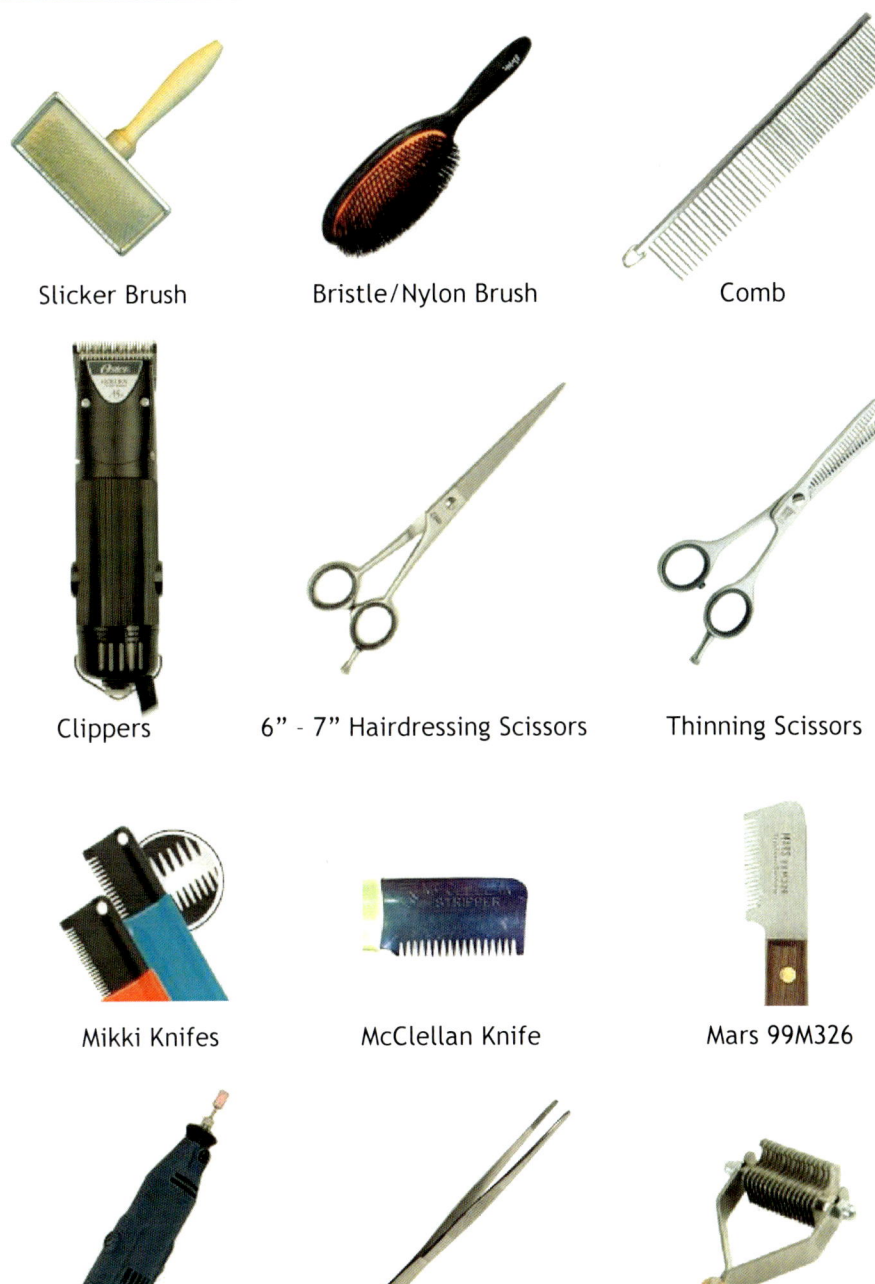

Slicker Brush   Bristle/Nylon Brush   Comb

Clippers   6" - 7" Hairdressing Scissors   Thinning Scissors

Mikki Knifes   McClellan Knife   Mars 99M326

Nail Grinder   Tweezers   Coat King

List of Advertisers

The Giant Schnauzer Club would like to thank all advertisers for their help in sponsoring the handbook:

Karen Carroll & Rick Latour - Ferncliffe

Mark & Clare Tyson - Tyshunde

Kirk Moss & Michelle Heinz - Riesenheim

Jack & Frances Krall - Jafrak

Helena Hutchings - Jenerelena

Sue Cox & Ken Bowman - Grovelea

Jo George - Daserbé

Norma Rylance - Foxwood

Mark, Jayne & Hannah Houchin - Barnsdale

Robert Joy & Neil Loach - Bellgard

Kevin & Sandie Cullen - Philoma

José Velhinho & George Donley - Echodream

Joe Conway - Lucavale

Elizabeth Lewis-Cracknell - Leadenpenny

Joy Lunn - Coldnose

Lesley & Jim Parker - Draxpark

Ferncliffe Schnauzers
Est 1987

We are a small, professional kennels of well bred, typical Schnauzers – all of excellent temperaments. We have several imported, sound, healthy bloodlines. Arguably the best genetic diversity in the country.

Ch Ferncliffe's Bete Noire

Ferncliffe Schnauzers
Est 1987

All puppies are K.C. registered, micro chipped eye tested (both parents hold a current, clear eye certificate), wormed, insured for 4 weeks and come with a full puppy pack, which includes information about the breed, diet, grooming and life long after care and, should the situation arise, there's always a home here at Ferncliffe.

Rus Astershvarc Revolution At Riesenheim (IMP RUS)

Est 1987

For those interested, give Karen or Rick a ring to arrange a visit to meet our dogs first-hand. There is never an obligation to buy. Inspected and Accredited by the Kennel Club. Inspected annually and Licensed by Lancaster City Council.

Hassanhill's Quorum
For Ferncliffe (IMP SWE)

Tyshunde Working Giant Schnauzers

Tyshunde Giant Schnauzers are originally from German Working lines with links to the Ferncliffe Kennel

Ferncliffe Quaid at Tyshunde (Rolf)

Our dogs are high drive, bold, confident with sound temperaments

Druminphilips Alida for Ferncliffe at Tyshunde (Ally)

Druminphilips Asterix for Ferncliffe (Alix)

Advice given on all aspects of working, training and obedience.
Personal Protection Dogs also available

Contact Mark or Clare Tyson

07736 433015   07742 008535

mark@tysonprotectiondogs.co.uk
www.tysonprotectiondogs.co.uk

Professional Grooming and Bathing Service Available. Phone: Clare

RIESENHEIM

Simply The Best

Photo taken 2 ½ Years

Ch Riesenheim Suited N'Booted For Daleiden

Top Giant Puppy 2004
B.I.S Giant Schnauzer Club Ch Show 2005
SCGB Puppy Of The Year 2005
SCGB Schnauzer Of The Year 2006
Top Giant 2006, 2007 & 2008
Crufts Best Of breed 2006
33 CC's
3 Working Group 1's & Over 20 Group Placings
Top Sire 2008
Top Stud 2009 & 2010

Nuts About Mutts
Our Online Shop

www.nutsaboutmutts.co.uk

Not Just A Show Dog!!!

RIESENHEIM

Photo taken 12 Months
Ch Riesenheim Capt Fantastic
B.I.S Giant Schnauzer Club Ch Show 2006
SCGB Schnauzer Of The Year 2007
GSC Top Puppy 2006

Photo taken 2 ½ Years
Ch Riesenheim Bite The Bullet
B.I.S Giant Schnauzer Club Ch Show 2009
B.I.S Northern Schnauzer Club Ch Show 2009
Top Giant Male 2009

Top Giant Schnauzer 2010
GSC

RIESENHEIM

The Future's Bright The Future's Riesenheim

PHOTO TAKEN 20 MONTHS
Riesenheim Gangsta Rap
SCGB Schnauzer Puppy Of The Year 2010

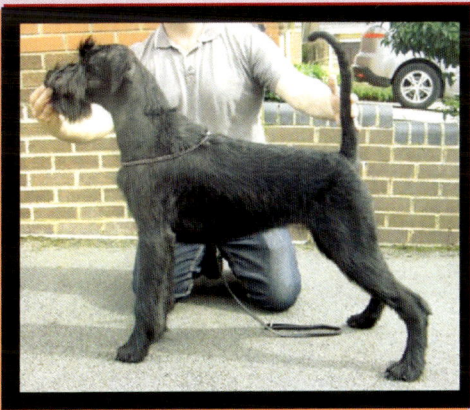

PHOTO TAKEN 6 MONTHS
Riesenheim Pistols At Dawn

Kirk & Michelle
01793 703909 WWW.RIESENHEIM.COM

Ch & Gib Ch Jafrak Le Fantasie

Jack & Frances Krall

Tel: 01984 667495
Email: contact@jafrak.com
www.jafrak.com

Nothing gives us more pleasure than to see others winning with our stock, we are always happy to sell a good one!
Of the many Champions bred here the following have become Champions for others, many of them novices and newcomers to Giants.

Ch Jafrak Annie Get Your Gun	Kay & Keith Roberts
Ch Jafrak Philadelphia	Kay & Keith Roberts
Ch Jafrak Brushstrokes	Rita Thomas
(The Bitch breed CC record holder & group winner)	
Ch Jafrak Zuchini	Audrey Heard
Ch Jafrak Dream Come True	Audrey Heard
Ch Jafrak Keep Talking	Caroline Wareing
Ch Jafrak Wheel Of Fortune	Gail & Martin Wise
Ch Jafrak Porcini	Maryse Faulkner
Ch Jafrak Dream On	Tina Crouch
Ch Jafrak See If I Care	Jenny Tucker
Ch Jafrak Philharmonica	Bernice Loving
Multi Ch Jafrak Earl Grey	Laurence Vincilioni
Ch Jafrak Dolcelata	Kevin & Sandie Cullen
(Group and Reserve Best In Show Winner)	
Ch Jafrak Philippe Olivier	Kevin & Sandie Cullen

(Top Dog all Breeds 2003, CC record holder, and ofcourse Best In Show **CRUFTS 2008**)

Jack & Frances Krall

Tel: 01984 667495
Email: contact@jafrak.com
www.jafrak.com

Jenerelena
Presents

JAFRAK PHILADELFIA FREEDOM Sh.CM

Although lightly shown Lola has had a lot of fun, not only has she achieved her show certificate of merit title, but has won numerous BOB, BP, group wins, puppy group wins, best in show and best puppy in show awards.

This was topped by her **Reserve Challenge Certificate at CRUFTS 2010** (Judge Mr A Fletcher), a day we will never forget and would like to thank Mr Fletcher for thinking so highly of our girl.

Thanks also go to Jack and Frances Krall for breeding Lola and giving us such wonderful support.

Owned and adored by Helena Hutchings & Keith Brooks
Handled by Helena Hutchings
Photo by Keith Brooks
c/o 5 Maple Drive, Firsdown, Salisbury, SP5 1SY
Tel – 01980 863744 e-mail jenerelena@aol.com, www.jenerelena.com

GROVELEA

In 1984 ... It Started with ... Emilie and Isabelle...

With thanks to the Sandridge kennel for their help and encouragement ... teaching me about Schnauzer type.

GROVELEA

In 1984...it started ... A love affair with the Giant Schnauzer

Along the way came Grovelea Barnstormer 1989 - 2004

GROVELEA

In 1984... it started ... As the years rolled by, no turning back...

The dearest friend Fleur
Many more Giants down the years, all special and full of memories.

GROVELEA

*In 1984……… it started with a kiss………
And you climbed into my heart*

*Along the years keeping the faith, and striving to breed quality 'typey',
'honest', Giant Schnauzers. And never forgetting that although they
have been my breed all this time, some day soon they will be someone
else's and they will carry on the dream.*

**Sue Cox & Ken Bowman
Westholm, Sheerwater, Ash, Canterbury, Kent. CT3 2LJ.
Tel 01304 813973
Email Grovelea@aol.com website www.freewebs.com/grovelea**

DASERBÉ
GIANT SCHNAUZERS

We are a small select kennel based in South Wales.
We have owned/exhibited and only selectively bred this lovely breed for almost 20 years.

Scapman's Valaraukar Von Daserbe (Imp Fra) Shcm

Proven at stud

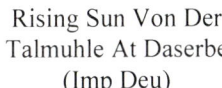

Rising Sun Von Der Talmuhle At Daserbe (Imp Deu)

We have recently imported new bloodlines into this country in the form of our French bred male and our German bred female.
All of our dogs are regularly health screened.

Mrs J George
Glamorgan
South Wales
02920 651640 daserbe-dogs@hotmail.com

Foxwood
Giants of distinction

Norma Rylance

Tele: 01302 860883   Mobile: 07867 555 727

Foxwood

Giants of reputation

Norma Rylance

E: foxwoodgiants@talktalk.net   www.foxwoodgiants.com

Barnsdale Schnauzers
Fit For Purpose Fit For Life

Barnsdale Designer Made By Foxwood: Handled By Miss Hannah Houchin

Telephone +44 (0) 1226 203981

Email Barnsdale@blueyonder.co.uk

www.barnsdalegiantschnauzers.co.uk

Bellgard Giant Schnauzers
Health, Temperament & Beauty as Standard

Black and Pepper & Salt

Champion Bellgard Ghetto Stiletto
Schnauzer of the Year 2009

Robert Joy & Neil Loach
Stoney Stanton
Leicestershire
01455 273915 / 07515 594415
www.bellgardgiants.co.uk

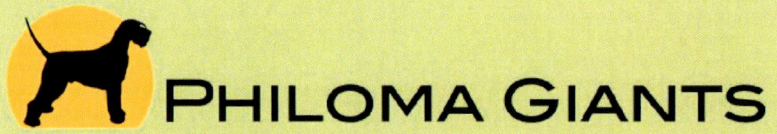
PHILOMA GIANTS

PHILOMA GHETTO CALIPSO
AT SIX MONTHS

Best Puppy in Show Schnauzer Club of Great Britain's 80th Anniversary show, 6 Best Puppy in Breed, Puppy Group 2 at Bath, Puppy Group 1 at Bournemouth, 1 CC, 2 res CC's

Contact: Kevin and Sandie Cullen
Tele: 01424 752815
Email: giants@philoma.com
www.philoma.com

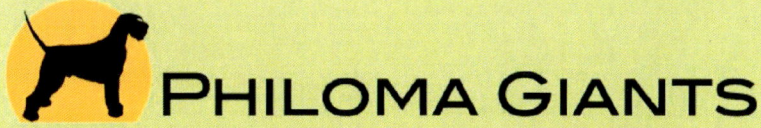

PHILOMA GIANTS

PHILOMA HIGH TIME

Best puppy in show N.W.P.B, Pro Plan Dog World Pup of the Year heat winner, 2 res CC's at only nine months

Contact: Kevin and Sandie Cullen
Tele: 01424 752815
Email: giants@philoma.com
www.philoma.com

Echodream
Giant Schnauzers

Mr. Jose Velhinho & Mr. George Donley

Puppies Occasionally Available to permanent Homes
www.echodream.co.uk
Email: contact@echodream.co.uk

Surrey

Photo by Steph Holbrook

PEPPER & SALT GIANT SCHNAUZERS
BLACK SCHNAUZERS

HEALTH & TEMPERAMENTS PARAMOUNT

MR J M D CONWAY
01945 861862

LEADENPENNY
Pepper and Salt
Giant Schnauzers

The Old Stables, Dunwich, Suffolk, IP17 3DW   01728 648653
lewiscracknell@dsl.pipex.com

Eye tested, hip scored, DNA profiled

Sometimes puppies are available, reared in the home as part of the family, carefully bred for health, vigour, genetic diversity and temperament.

Three Leadenpenny generations amongst the fir-cones

Swimming in the North Sea

Caravaggio

COLDNOSE

Breeders of top quality Giant Schnauzers
and Black & Silver Miniature Schnauzers

Con Amore da Felmor to Coldnose (imp Italy) DOB 05.06.04
(Ch. Savali Bodyguard Zovely-N ex Ch. Luna-N Degli Ussari Neri)

From the best European bloodlines, this top quality dog is beautifully constructed with an outstanding temperament. Luca is siring healthy puppies of excellent type, quality and temperament from our top Scandinavian and European bloodlines.

JOY LUNN
UK and FRANCE +44 (0) 7976 597984
www.coldnose.co.uk   joy@coldnose.co.uk

European import/export service available.

COLDNOSE

Acknowledgements

The Giant schnauzer club would like to thank all those fellow enthusiasts who have written articles and provided photographs and information for this handbook.

Special thanks are extended to Lesley Parker who has worked tirelessly with the help of her husband Jim and Karen Carroll to produce this handbook.
Without them this book would not have been possible.

Bibliography

Lemish, Michael G (1996). *War Dogs; A History of Loyalty and Heroism*, USA, Brasseys Inc.

Gallant, J (1996) *The World of Schnauzers*, Alpine Publications

Military Working Dog Foundation. 2002, Caring For America's Canine Heroes: History [online] Available at: www.militaryworkingdogs.com/history.shtml [accessed 20/4/2010]

The Giant Schnauzer Club (1999). The Giant Schnauzer Club Handbook

The Giant Schnauzer Club (1989). The Giant Schnauzer Club Handbook

Stahlkuppe, J (2002). Giant Schnauzers: A Complete Pet Owner's Manual, NY Barron's Educational Series, Inc.

Andrews, B J (2000). Giant Schnauzer: Special Rare Breed Edition, Surrey, Interpet

The Kennel Club (1998-2010). Breed Records Supplement to the Stud Book

The Kennel Club (1974-1980). Breed Records Supplement to the Stud Book

Hilterscheld, Sara. The History & Development of the Giant Schnauzer, NZKC Supplement 31

BVA (01/2010). The British Veterinary Association/Kennel Club/International Sheep Dog Society (BVA/KC/ISDS) Eye Scheme: What is the Eye Scheme. BVA